A CRITICAL STUDY
OF ACCOUNTING FOR
BUSINESS COMBINATIONS

ACCOUNTING
RESEARCH
STUDY NO. 5

A CRITICAL STUDY OF ACCOUNTING FOR BUSINESS COMBINATIONS

By Arthur R. Wyatt, Ph.D., CPA
Professor of Accountancy
University of Illinois

AMERICAN
INSTITUTE
OF CPAs

Copyright 1963, by the
American Institute of Certified Public Accountants
666 Fifth Ave., New York 19, N. Y.

This research study is published for discussion purposes. It does not represent the official position of the American Institute of Certified Public Accountants.

Table of Contents

	Page
LIST OF COMPANIES CITED	ix
DIRECTOR'S PREFACE	xi
AUTHOR'S PREFACE	xv

Chapter

1. THE BUSINESS COMBINATION PHENOMENON 1
    The First Merger Period, 2
    The Second Merger Period, 3
    The Recent Merger Period, 4
    Motivations in the Recent Merger Period—the
        Selling or Absorbed Company, 6
        Tax consequences, 6
        Diversification, 6
        Profit, 6
        Retirement, 6
    Factors Motivating the Buying or Absorbing Company, 7
        Tax consequences, 7
        Growth or expansion, 7
        Diversification, 8
        Financial considerations, 8
        Competitive pressures, 8
    Influence of Antitrust Legislation, 8
    Types of Business Combinations, 9

2. THE NATURE AND SIGNIFICANCE OF THE PROBLEM . . 11
    The Research Plan, 12
    A Brief Look at the Problem Area, 13
    A Brief Look at Related Issues, 16
    The Problem Area in Perspective, 17

3. ACCOUNTING FOR BUSINESS COMBINATIONS PRIOR TO 1949   19
    The Earned Surplus Question, 20
    "Pooling of Interests"—A New Term Emerges, 22
    Pooling of Interests—Early AICPA Reference, 23
    Accounting Research Bulletin No. 40, 24

Chapter	Page

4. ACCOUNTING FOR SPECIFIC BUSINESS COMBINATIONS . . 26
   Combinations Reviewed—Size Relationship, 27
   Examples of Small Poolings, 28
   Accounting for Assets, 30
   Accounting for Earned Surplus, 32
   Summary—Accounting Aspects, 33
   Criteria for Determining the Nature of the Combination, 35
   Continuity of Ownership Interests, 35
   Continuance of Acquired Company as a Subsidiary, 37
   Classification of Transaction, 37
   The Problem of Intangibles, 38
   Income Tax Influence, 39
   Summary, 41

5. DISCLOSURE OF BUSINESS COMBINATIONS IN ANNUAL
   REPORTS 43
   Disclosure for "Pooled" Combinations, 43
   Disclosure for "Purchased" Combinations, 44
   Disclosure of Nature of the Transaction, 45
   Recasting of Preceding Year Data, 46
   Recasting Five- to Ten-Year Summaries, 48
   Retroactive Change, 49
   *Reporting Requirements Under Accounting Research
      Bulletin No. 48, 53*
   Summary, 54

6. THE PRESENT DILEMMA 56
   The Pooling-of-Interests Concept, 56
   *Forces Acting to Promote Use of the Pooling
      Treatment, 57*
   The Significance of Accounting for Goodwill, 58
   Changing Pattern of Pooling Concept, 61
   Goodwill, 62
   Retained Earnings (Earned Surplus), 64
   Retroactive Poolings, 66

7. ACCOUNTING FOR BUSINESS COMBINATIONS—TOWARD A
   SOLUTION 68
   The Nature of a Business Combination, 69
   Peculiarities of Business Combinations, 70
   The Criteria, 73
   Accounting for Assets Received, 74
      Purchase accounting, 74

Chapter	Page

    Pooling accounting, 76
    Summary, 77
  Accounting for Consideration Given, 77
    Purchase accounting, 77
    Pooling accounting, 79
    Summary, 80
  The Fair Value Pooling Concept, 81

**8. ACCOUNTING FOR BUSINESS COMBINATIONS—
CONSEQUENCES OF ALTERNATIVES** **87**
  Consequences of Purchase Accounting, 87
    Goodwill, 87
    Dilution of earnings per share, 88
    Emphasis on market value per share, 91
    Nonhomogeneous asset valuations, 91
    Retained earnings, 92
  Consequences of Pooling Accounting, 92
    Goodwill write-off, 92
    Asset misstatement, 93
    Earnings per share, 94
    Bargaining position, 95
  *Problems Arising from Adoption of Purchase
    Accounting, 96*
    Determination of fair value, 96
    Bargain purchases, 97
    Amortization of goodwill, 98
  *Problems Arising from Adoption of Pooling
    Accounting, 98*
    Part cash and part securities, 98
    Multi-step combinations, 100
    Part preferred shares and part common shares, 101
    Minority interests, 102

9. CONCLUSIONS AND RECOMMENDATIONS **103**
  Conclusions, 104
  Recommendations, 105

ANOTHER LOOK AT BUSINESS COMBINATIONS **109**

APPENDIX **115**
  ARB No. 24—Accounting for Intangible Assets, 115
  ARB No. 40—Business Combinations, 123
  ARB No. 43, Chapter 5—Intangible Assets, 127

ARB No. 43, Chapter 7c—Business Combinations, 131
ARB No. 48—Business Combinations, 134

SELECTED BIBLIOGRAPHY 140

INDEX 144

List of Companies Cited

Company	Page
Aluminum Company of America	51, 52
American Machine & Foundry Company	49, 50, 51
American Smelting and Refining Company	2
Bell & Howell Company	47, 48
Caterpillar Tractor Co.	24, 29
Celanese Corporation of America	24
Food Machinery and Chemical Corporation	53
General Telephone & Electronics Corporation	44
Glen Alden Corporation	47
The May Department Stores	48
G. C. Murphy	32
National City Lines Inc.	45
The Ohio Oil Company	45
Pullman Incorporated	46
Raytheon Company	52, 53
Rexall Drug and Chemical Company	47
Standard Oil Company	2
Sunray Mid-Continent Oil Company	46
Union Carbide and Carbon Corporation	29, 30
Union Tank Car Company	47
United States Steel Corporation	2

Director's Preface

In this study, Arthur Wyatt has made a substantial contribution to our knowledge of the way in which accounting practices and principles are formed. He presents us with a careful, detailed, documented analysis of the interrelationships among (1) the combination movement in the U.S. in recent decades, (2) business policy, (3) the tax law, and (4) accounting principles as expressed primarily in the bulletins of the committee on accounting procedure of the American Institute of Certified Public Accountants. The general conclusion is unavoidable that accounting for business combinations has deteriorated in recent years so that a variety of practices can be described as "accepted."

In his analysis of the facts he has found, Arthur Wyatt says in effect that in the vast majority of cases (those in which a large company absorbs a small one) the transaction should be interpreted as a purchase by the larger company of the assets of the smaller, regardless of the specific form of the transaction and regardless of the type of consideration used. His two key recommendations flow logically from this "purchase" emphasis: (a) to use fair values at date of acquisition for the assets, and (b) not to bring forward the retained earnings of the smaller company. The proposed solution, however, assumes an answer to a key question—what is "the entity" for which the accounting is being made?

Arthur Wyatt indentifies "the entity" with the legal unit which survives to carry on business activities after a business combination has occurred. In a key paragraph, appearing early in chapter 7 (page 69), he states:

> In looking for the nature of a business combination we must recognize that it can take many forms. But, regardless of the form, a business combination occurs when one company acquires, assumes, or otherwise gains control over the assets or properties of another company by an exchange of assets or equities, or when two companies of equal size merge to form a new enterprise.

> Thus a business combination is essentially a particular type of business transaction.

The definition incorporated in the preceding quotation then leads naturally to a discussion of business transactions in general and to the business combination in particular as a special type of business transaction.

Suppose, however, that a business combination is defined as follows:

> A business combination occurs when two or more companies merge their assets or place them under common ownership or control by any one of a variety of methods.

In this definition the emphasis is on the merger of assets and on common ownership or control.

In order to make some progress in assessing the practical consequences of the preceding definitions, Robert C. Holsen, CPA, agreed to study the problem. His report appears on pages 109 to 114 under the title, "Another Look at Business Combinations." I concur with his conclusions that "... a purchase occurs when ... one group ... gives up its ownership interest in the assets it formerly controlled," that "... a pooling ... occurs when equity shares are exchanged ..." and that "... criteria such as relative size and continuity of management ..." are neither logical nor practical guides to a distinction between a purchase and a pooling. His discussion of the specific meaning of "an exchange of shares" is to the point and should supply the business community with a sound basis for interpreting the nature of a merger.

Mr. Holsen concludes his report with some comments on intangible assets, with special reference to goodwill. The problem of the proper valuation of assets, tangible or intangible, is a broad one but is separate and distinct from the problem of an appropriate interpretation of a business combination. I therefore take no stand in connection with this study on his proposal with respect to goodwill but I do agree that the whole area of accounting for goodwill needs re-examination.

Hassel Tippit, a member of the Accounting Principles Board, acted as chairman of a project advisory committee whose members were John C. Biegler, Joel Hunter, William J. Ivey, John Peoples, and Phillip L. West. This committee reviewed the plan of the study in its early stages and commented on the various drafts of the report both in person and in correspondence. The committee members assisted Arthur Wyatt and others on my staff in many ways. The committee takes no responsibility for the study itself. The only positive obligation imposed on them was to advise me as to the suitability of the manuscript for publication as a research study.

The committee is of the opinion that Professor Wyatt's study is good insofar as it relates to background material and general discussion, but some members feel that its conclusions and recommendations are not realistic and do not give adequate recognition to other points of view. The study seems to favor a discontinuance of almost all poolings of interests. The committee feels that the distinction between poolings and purchases should be continued, but with such modifications as are necessary in the criteria relating to the two forms of business combinations to make the distinction rest on differences of substance and not of form. Also, the committee is not disposed to accept the fair value approach to combinations of companies of approximately equal size. While certain members of the committee wish to receive judgment as to some of the specific details of Mr. Holsen's report, particularly as they relate to the use of treasury stock in a business combination, the committee generally concurs in the discussion and conclusions reached by Mr. Holsen in his report.

New York, N. Y., June 1963   MAURICE MOONITZ
                                                     Director of Accounting Research

Author's Preface

The Accounting Research Division of the American Institute of Certified Public Accountants approved a study of the accounting for business combinations in March 1960. The announcement indicated that "particular attention will be paid to the 'pooling-of-interest' approach to the problem and a survey will be made of the experience with this type of combination in recent years." This monograph is the result of research activities in these areas as well as consideration of the basic aspects of the combination transaction and their relation to basic postulates of accounting.

The members of a project advisory committee, under the chairmanship of Hassel Tippit of Cleveland, Ohio, served effectively as advisers and consultants during the conduct of the study. In addition, numerous certified public accountants and other interested individuals and firms made suggestions, comments, and criticisms which were most helpful in the final development of the monograph. To these people I extend my sincere thanks for the guidance and encouragement provided. Special acknowledgment is due officials of the New York Stock Exchange who were most co-operative and helpful in making materials from their files available for my use.

I am particularly grateful to Donald E. Kieso, instructor in accountancy at the University of Illinois, for his valuable assistance in accumulating the data on numerous combinations in the early phases of this study. In addition, his constructive analytical comments and criticisms on the various drafts of the monograph were particularly beneficial. I would also like to express my gratitude to Maurice Moonitz for his over-all guidance and constructive criticisms at various stages of the study. While these men and others were most helpful throughout the study, I must accept full responsibility for the conclusions drawn and the reasoning used to support them.

Urbana, Ill., June 1963   ARTHUR R. WYATT

1

The Business Combination Phenomenon

While interest in the accounting problems arising from business combinations has been intensified in the last twenty years, the business combination phenomenon is not a recent development on the American business scene. Combinations of business entities have occurred from the time that the corporate form of business organization became prominent. Ever since the passage of the Sherman Act in 1890, the Federal Government has attempted to regulate the combination movement by prohibiting those combinations in restraint of trade. Over the years, the legislative restraints have been extended, most notably in the Clayton Act of 1914, and the significant revision of that act in 1950.

Historically, three relatively distinct periods of merger or combination have occurred in the United States. The first wave of mergers falls in the years following the passage of the Sherman Act, from 1890 to 1904. This period has been called the classical era of consolidation. The main feature of the combinations of this period was the holding company, a corporate structure to control the operations of the various operating units falling within its framework. The holding company was typically not an operating unit, its assets consisting basically of its investment in the shares of a number of operating units, or possibly in subholding companies. The motivation behind the combinations of this period was relatively simple—the creation of vertical, fully integrated corporate complexes for the purpose of dominating the markets in which the units would operate. Many of the holding companies merely joined together organizations that were previously closely related. Typical of the corporate complexes of this era were Standard Oil Company, United States Steel Corporation, and American Smelting and Refining Company.

A second wave of mergers started about the end of World War I and continued through the 1920's. During this period the combinations effected were significantly smaller in relation to the economy as a whole than they had been in the earlier period. In general the combinations of this era involved piecemeal acquisitions designed principally to expand the operations of the dominant company.

The third wave of business combinations began with the end of World War II and continues in relatively full force at the present time. Actually, a significant spurt in merger activity is apparent during the late 1950's. As with the combinations in the second period, the more recent combinations have typically involved piecemeal acquisitions designed to strengthen a competitive position, to diversify into new market areas, or to keep abreast of the rapidly developing technological changes initiated by the war. Combinations of this third period have been even less significant on an individual basis in relation to the total economy than were the combinations of the second period. A closer look at some of the forces acting to stimulate the combination movement will bring out the rather sharp distinction among the combinations arising in these three periods.

The First Merger Period

The business combinations of the first period brought together in "partnership" the leading competitors in an industry. These combinations were unquestionably spurred by the rather chaotic market conditions and the widely swinging cyclical fluctuations in the economy during the period subsequent to the Civil War. The combinations effected during this period had as a clear objective the development of a monopoly position from which the pattern of prices could be established. Likewise, the newly dominant enterprise framed the ground rules under which the fringe or marginal members of the industry could operate.

The combinations of this period were brought together largely as the result of the efforts of the investment bankers. The combinations were characterized by relatively complex corporate structures, in many cases with several layers of operating and holding companies. Likewise, in the opinion of many at the time, the shares issued to effect some of these combinations were considerably watered because the acquiring company (frequently a holding company) issued a greater dollar amount of par value stock than the tangible net assets acquired were worth, either in terms of book value or market value. (During this period the normal basis of accounting for the properties involved in the combinations was the par value of the stock given in the exchange.)

The impact of the combinations of this first merger period was considerable.

> By [1900] over 300 industrial combinations representing consolidations of about 5000 distinct plants and covering most major lines of productive industry, had been formed. Authoritative estimates indicate that these combinations controlled fully 40% of the manufacturing capital of the country with 78 of these consolidated corporations controlling one half or more of the country's total production in their respective fields and with 26 controlling 80% or more.[1]

The Second Merger Period

Much of the impetus for the mergers in the second period likewise came from bankers. The public was in a growth and speculative mood, which made the launching of mergers relatively easy. The existence of stringent antimonopoly laws, however, kept the already large corporations out of this movement relative to their participation in the earlier one. While many large corporate complexes resulted from combinations of this period, the new corporations did not in general achieve the dominance of an industry attained in the former era.

Considerably more importance also appears to have been attached in this second period to the internal organization and management of the resultant corporations. While investment bankers were still the promoters of many of the combinations, the managements of the constituent enterprises were now better qualified to participate in the merger negotiations and to foresee in advance the problems which would emerge subsequent to the merger. As a result a greater proportion of the combinations of this period weathered the cyclical fluctuations of the economy and prospered through the depression of the early 1930's.

Many of the promotional efforts of the second merger period, how-

---

[1] J. Keith Butters, John Lintner, and William L. Cary, *Effects of Taxation; Corporate Mergers,* p. 288. 1951.

ever, also overstepped the bounds of financial soundness. Once again allegations were made that the resultant corporate complex had watered its stock and overstated its asset values. Some of these promotional extravaganzas came to grief with the impact of the depression.

The Recent Merger Period

The more recent period of mergers has characteristics somewhat different from those of the earlier periods. First, the initiators of most of the recent mergers are the operating executives of industry rather than the investment bankers so prominent in the earlier periods. A wider variety of business motivations appears to support the numerous mergers of this period, with most of these related to business expectations of considerable economic growth in the future.

Few of the combinations in this period involve two major corporations. The general pattern of combination involves either two corporations of relatively the same size, neither of which is dominant in its industry, or two corporations so disproportionate in size that the resultant company is not materially different immediately after the combination from what it was before. Subsequent to the merger, however, significant changes in the corporate make-up might arise because of the combination.

A number of other forces have been at work to enhance the trend toward combination. As business expanded following World War II a shortage of superior managerial ability became evident. Companies with faltering or relatively ineffective managerial personnel became fair merger prospects. As wage rates increased and labor costs tended to absorb a larger share of the sales dollar, technological innovations gained prominence. Companies soon found, however, that the research behind innovation was costly and the savings from newly developed techniques could be profitable only when applied to a greater scale of operations. Thus, business combinations were sought both to provide the necessary capital for research and to achieve a broader base upon which to employ the innovations developed.

Another apparently significant consideration was the income tax. The number of combinations either directly or primarily attributable to tax-law provisions can be questioned, but there is little question that in the otherwise favorable climate, the provisions of the tax law acted as a stimulus to combination. Many family-held or closely held corporations had become extremely profitable, and their owners were approaching retirement. The provisions of the tax law which permit postponement of taxes in certain "tax-free" exchanges of stock encouraged the merger of these corporations into other, generally larger, more widely owned corporate structures.

A number of other motivations appeared in specific combination situations, such as the opportunity to broaden operations by the addition of new products, the opportunity to reduce costs, to improve competitive position, etc. The important feature of the combinations in this third period, however, was the desire of some managements to capitalize on what appeared to be unusually good growth prospects coupled with a desire of other managements to relinquish their positions, to become part of a stronger unit, or to strengthen their personal positions preparatory to retirement.

One result of the different environment in which these mergers were effected is the relative absence of allegations that watered stock or overstated asset values have emerged from the combination transaction.

> The securities laws of the 1930's have had such a dampening effect on exuberant promoters that it would be hard to find a merger today where the stock has been casually watered. To be sure, some merged securities have been over valued, particularly in growth industries, but this bidding up of values has been done largely by speculators dazzled by the growth possibilities in chemicals, oils, air conditioning, or electronics. The securities offered were not inflated when they were first offered by the businessman traders who put them together. This tough, barrelhead trading between managers for the purpose of buying time, betting on the future, fighting for lower costs, struggling for the security of size, or for the many other reasons driving them into deals is the principal characteristic of today's merger movement.[2]

Whereas in the earlier periods the use of par value as the basis of recording the combination transaction may have produced some instances of watered stock and overstated asset values, accounting in the third merger period was considerably more conservative. The two widely used methods of recording business combinations in this recent merger period, "purchases" or "poolings," will be described more fully in the following chapter. Neither of these accounting methods attaches significance to par value. Likewise, as will be noted in subsequent chapters, the pooling treatment may well create the antithesis of watered stock, namely, secret reserves. At any rate, acounting for the

---

[2] William B. Harris, "The Urge to Merge," *Fortune*, Nov. 1954, p. 242.

more recent combinations has been far more conservative than was the accounting for similar combinations in earlier periods.

Motivations in the Recent Merger Period—
the Selling or Absorbed Company

Tax consequences. Income tax considerations are apparently a strongly motivating force for business entities which sell out or are absorbed in a business combination. If a company enters into a business combination, the burden of estate taxes on the owners may be lessened; distributions to owners can be made at capital gains rates; and operating-loss carryovers which might otherwise be lost may be utilized.

Diversification. The stockholder-owner-manager of a closely held business may desire either to retire and diversify his assets, or to diversify his assets even though continuing to serve the company or unit with which he has been associated. Not infrequently an individual, after a number of years of hard work, realizes that his wealth is contingent upon the success of one business entity. Through a combination with another corporation he will receive stock which has a ready market. He can then proceed to diversify his holdings, if he wishes, by disposing of his stock in an orderly fashion, without peril to the business itself.

Profit. The stockholder may be motivated to sell his business because he is offered an attractive price.

Retirement. The stockholder may decide to sell his business simply because he wishes to retire and has no one to whom to convey the business. In such a situation a combination effected by means of an exchange of stock may be advantageous from an income tax viewpoint. Rather than recognizing any gain immediately, as would be the case in a sale for cash, the seller may recognize his gain during retirement by selling periodically a portion of the stock received in exchange.

While any or all of these factors may be present in a given combination in varying degrees, the tax incentives appear paramount as far as the seller is concerned. This position is not, however, shared by all investigators. Butters, Lintner, and Cary, for example, found that tax pressures definitely exerted strong pressure on owners of many closely held businesses to sell, but they concluded that taxes probably had received more prominence than was warranted as the reason behind the actual sale of businesses. Even in their analysis, however, tax incentives at least supplement and support the other reasons for owners of closely held businesses to sell out to other companies.[3]

Factors Motivating the Buying or Absorbing Company

Tax consequences. Butters, Lintner, and Cary found that tax consequences were of little or no significance in motivating the purchasing or absorbing company in a business combination.[4] However, it does appear likely that in the past some acquisitions of companies possessing operating-loss carryovers were motivated in part by the benefits to accrue from the use of these deductions.

Growth or expansion. The desire for growth motivates many business executives today. Growth may involve the development of a new product, the acquisition of new or additional productive capacity, the acquisition of new sources of supply or of strategic market outlets. Expansion by combination has certain advantages over expansion by construction of new facilities to accomplish the expansion program; a combination of this type does not intensify competition as does the construction of facilities in addition to those already in production. It also provides ready markets which might otherwise take years to develop, and can frequently be consummated with greater speed and certainty than can growth through construction of new facilities.

Growth may also be motivated to a varying degree by the personal goals of the executive. Executives with only a small ownership interest recognize that their future status may depend in large measure on the prestige and power which they can accumulate. Actions which tend to enlarge or expand the company also tend to increase the power and prestige of the executives.

> Behind the publicly stated or "good" reason [for a business combination] often lurks the "real" reason. The real reason may actually be the very kinetic energy of management, which operates on the theory that each succeeding year must show an im-

---

[3] J. Keith Butters, John Lintner, and William L. Cary, *Effects of Taxation; Corporate Mergers,* p. 27. 1951.
[4] *Ibid.,* p. 212.

provement over the preceding year as measured by sales, assets, and earnings.[5]

Diversification. Competitive conditions often stimulate entry into new fields in order to control sources of supply or to assure market outlets. Likewise, development of new products may stimulate one company to seek out another with productive facilities available to permit development of the new product. Acquisitions which accomplish diversification may also have at their source a desire to smooth cyclical or seasonal patterns. In some instances, declining markets for existing products indicate a need to find "something new" in order to utilize the physical facilities and the work force of the company.

Financial considerations. Some companies find themselves at a competitive disadvantage when it comes to obtaining additional capital because of their lack of size or prominence in the financial community. Thus, business combinations may be stimulated by the desire to provide a foundation to support additional growth through addition of facilities or to support additional short-term borrowing to permit fuller development of existing facilities.

Competitive pressures. In many industries the emphasis on growth gradually produces an increasingly competitive market situation. Those smaller companies which may have a competitive advantage are sought after to provide a means of alleviating the competitive pressure. The economies anticipated in a larger scale operation become more crucial as competitive pressure increases. In this same group would be combinations effected in order to reduce costs.

Influence of Antitrust Legislation

The preceding discussion would indicate that the tax law provisions relating to corporate reorganizations have promoted, or at least have not restrained, business combinations in recent years. By contrast, however, the provisions of other Federal legislation and regulation have not been so favorable to business combinations.

The first statute of consequence dealing with antitrust and restriction of competition was the Sherman Act of 1890. This act made illegal any contracts, combinations, or conspiracies by which persons or com-

---

[5] Edgar T. Mead, Jr., "Mergers — Good Medicine or Bad?" pp. 31-32, in *Mergers and Acquisitions,* American Management Association, Inc. 1957.

panies restrained trade or by which they would combine with others to create monopolistic positions. Many acquisitions and mergers, however, as well as other contracts among businesses, fell short of being actionable under the Sherman Act, even though they tended to create monopolistic positions or otherwise restrain or lessen competition. Thus, in 1914 the Clayton Act was passed to prohibit price discrimination, exclusive dealing or tying contracts, and acquisitions of corporate stock where such activities might lead to serious impairment of competition in the markets affected.

By 1950 a modification of the Clayton Act was enacted to meet the shift in methods by which transfers of corporate control were effected. Instead of acquiring corporate stock in the combination transaction, corporations were acquiring the assets of other companies, the real effect of which was the same as if the combination had been effected through an exchange of stock. The 1950 Act prevented one corporation from acquiring another through acquisition of its assets, if it would have been prohibited under the 1914 Act from acquiring its stock.

The existence of Federal laws designed to prevent the lessening of competition, however, has not been effective in controlling the phenomenon, to any appreciable extent, principally because many of the combinations have not substantially lessened competition and many others have involved social consequences that are desirable. Acquisitions and mergers

> ... may lead to socially desirable developments to the extent that they increase efficiency in production and distribution, or simply reflect a free and competitive market for used fixed assets. But they may also lead to undesirable results in that they may restrain or eliminate competition or tend toward monopoly in particular lines of goods or services. The methods used provide no *per se* basis for evaluating the effects of corporate acquisitions on the public interest.[6]

Types of Business Combinations

Our review of business combinations consummated subsequent to World War II disclosed a wide diversity in the manner of effecting the combinations. However, most of the combinations reviewed fell into one of several "typical" patterns, the forms of which will be described below.

---

[6] U. S. Federal Trade Commission, *Report on Corporate Mergers and Acquisitions*, pp. 9-10. July 1955.

CHAPTER 1: THE BUSINESS COMBINATION PHENOMENON

1. Acquiring Company A issued voting stock for all the *voting stock* of the acquired Company B, with one company, A, resulting.

2. Acquiring Company A issued voting stock for all of the *voting stock* of the acquired Company B with both companies remaining in existence.

3. Acquiring Company A issued voting stock for the *assets* of the acquired Company B, with B either being liquidated shortly thereafter through a distribution of shares of A to B's shareholders or remaining in existence as an investment company.

4. Acquiring Company A issued voting stock and other equity claims and/or assets in exchange for the stock of acquired Company B, with one company, A, resulting.

5. Acquiring Company A issued voting stock and other equity claims and/or assets in exchange for the stock of acquired Company B with both companies remaining in existence.

6. A new company C was formed and issued its voting stock in exchange for all the voting stock of both A and B. New Company C might have a name different from A or B or might have the same name as either of these companies.

Many of these combinations were effected under applicable state statutes so that they qualified as statutory mergers. One other form of combination, which was rather prevalent and with which we were not particularly concerned, involved the payment in cash or other assets by the acquiring Company A in exchange for the stock or assets of Company B. Such a transaction is clearly a purchase by one company of the stock or properties of another company, the basis of accounting for which would be the cost to the acquiring company of the stock or assets acquired, as measured by the fair value of the assets given in exchange or at the fair value of the property acquired, whichever is more clearly evident. While combinations falling within this pattern were not emphasized in this study, the accounting for them was found to provide the basis of accounting used for some of the other types of combinations. Likewise, the accounting problems arising from combinations effected in this manner were also present in many combinations effected through exchanges of stock. These problems will be considered later in this study.

2

The Nature and Significance of the Problem

In a study of any area of accounting, it is quite difficult to isolate certain problems to the exclusion of others. In the study of business combinations we are primarily concerned with the accounting concepts to be used as guides in recording the effects of financial transactions and with the nature of informative disclosures in the financial statements. We are not primarily concerned with the other functions an accountant might perform in the business combination area, such as advice on the determination of exchange ratios, on appropriate valuation of assets, on the integration of management personnel, on records control mechanisms, and the like.

Although business combinations may take many forms, we are primarily concerned with those combinations that resulted from exchanges of stock interests. Thus, the emphasis is on the type of transaction in which Company A acquires all of the stock (or assets and properties) of Company B in exchange for shares of Company A's stock. Company B may either be dissolved or continued as a wholly owned subsidiary of Company A. Other forms of business combinations are not excluded, but the type just described is by far the most common one studied.

Business combinations are described in a variety of ways in accounting and business literature. Thus, we find references to mergers, consolidations, amalgamations, acquisitions, poolings of interests, as well as others. Each of these terms has had a precise meaning at some point in its usage, a meaning that has generally become obscured through overlapping usage. In this report the term "business combination" is used in a broad sense to include any transaction whereby one economic unit obtains control over the assets and properties of another economic unit, regardless of the legal avenue by which such control is obtained and regardless of the resultant form of the economic unit emerging from the combination transaction.

The area of business combinations produces accounting difficulties because of the wide variety in *form* which the transaction may take and because many combinations are effected without the existence of a definite objective basis for determining the dollar magnitudes involved in the transaction. Thus, an accountant, when faced with the necessity of recording the effect of a business combination, must decide whether the form of the transaction indicates what has taken place or whether the form masks the substantive features of the transaction. In addition, he needs some definite dollar value to use in recording the event. This latter point has been the one posing difficult problems in recent years.

The Research Plan

The initial phase of the research involved a study and review of the available literature dealing with the broad area of business combinations in general, and with the problems of accounting for them in particular. We reviewed background material dealing with such subjects as antitrust regulation, restraint of trade, early merger movements in the United States, and Federal income tax regulations pertaining to this area, in addition to the technical accounting literature.

The most extensive portion of the research effort was devoted to a study of the data available for a number of business combinations. Combinations studied were segregated by three time periods: (1) 1949-52, the period immediately preceding and following the issuance of *Accounting Research Bulletin No. 40*,[1] the initial pronouncement of the committee on accounting procedure of the American Institute of Certified Public Accountants in the business combination area; (2) 1954-56, the period following the issuance of *Accounting Research Bulletin No. 43*, in which Chapter 7c[2] contained a revision of the

---

[1] Reproduced in Appendix, p. 123.
[2] Reproduced in Appendix, p. 131.

previous *Bulletin No. 40;* and (3) 1958-60, the period following the issuance of *Accounting Research Bulletin No. 48*,[3] the most recent bulletin on accounting for business combinations.

For the first two of these periods the data available for review consisted of listing applications filed with the New York Stock Exchange, proxy statements or prospectuses submitted to shareholders in connection with the business combination, and annual reports. For the third period mentioned, in addition to the above data, we also examined letters filed with the Exchange by the independent accountants approving the accounting treatment proposed to be accorded the transaction by the acquiring or emerging company.

Several of the combinations studied in this phase of the research were selected for additional consideration. In general these combinations contained unusual features or were accorded unusual accounting treatment. For several of these combinations, discussions were held with representatives of the accounting firms that approved the accounting treatment. In addition, we discussed the problem area with representatives of a number of accounting firms, as well as other interested parties.

Annual reports of corporations involved in business combinations in the 1958-60 period were reviewed to determine the reporting treatment accorded those combinations. In addition, news releases and other published reports provided the source of significant information.

The final phase of the research program involved the consideration of the significant accounting features of business combinations, as disclosed through the earlier phases of the research, in conjunction with those aspects of accounting theory pertinent to the combination area. The basic postulates and broad principles of accounting were studied in the search for a solution to the problems in the business combination area.

A Brief Look at the Problem Area

If the terms of the combination provide that cash or other assets will be given in exchange for the stock or assets acquired, the acquiring company accounts for the stock or assets acquired at an amount equal to the cash or cash equivalent values of the assets given in exchange or at the fair value of the property acquired, whichever

---

[3] Reproduced in Appendix, p. 134.

is more clearly evident.[4] Thus, assume that Company B has assets with a book value of $1 million, liabilities of $200,000, and capital stock and retained earnings of $800,000. If Company A acquires all of the stock of Company B (or acquires all the assets and assumes all the liabilities) for cash or other assets totaling $1,250,000, Company A would normally account for the stock (or assets and liabilities) at a value of $1,250,000. This treatment is squarely in accord with the basis used in accounting for other acquisitions of assets or property under the generally accepted practice of accounting for assets initially on the basis of their cost to the acquiring company.

If the business combination is effected through an exchange of stock of Company A for the stock (or assets and liabilities) of Company B, the problem of valuation becomes more difficult. During the 1950's two alternative accounting treatments were followed. One method, generally called "purchase accounting," would account for the stock or assets acquired or controlled at an amount equal to the cash or cash equivalent value of the stock given in exchange, or at the fair value of the property acquired. Most commonly the basis used was the cash equivalent of the stock given in exchange, the "cash equivalent" being measured by the fair market value of the stock at some date reasonably close to the effective date of the combination, or at the average market price for an appropriate period preceding the combination. If the fair value of the assets acquired was used as the basis of accounting, the value was commonly determined by an appraisal of the various properties involved.

The other method, commonly called "pooling-of-interests accounting," would account for the stock or assets acquired or controlled at an amount equal to the book value of the stock or assets on the accounting records of the company being acquired or controlled. Thus, in the preceding example, the use of the "pooling" method would result in a value of $1 million for the assets acquired, and $200,000 for the liabilities, or a value of $800,000 for the net assets. If the "purchase" method were used, and if the fair value of the stock given (or if the assets acquired) were $1,250,000, the assets acquired would be valued at $1,450,000, and the liabilities at $200,000, or a value of $1,250,000 for the net assets. The accounting method used clearly has a material effect upon the resultant dollar ascriptions in the records.

---

[4] American Institute of Certified Public Accountants, Committee on Accounting Procedure, *Accounting Research Bulletin No. 48*, "Business Combinations," p. 24. Jan. 1957. (Reproduced in Appendix, p. 134.)

The "pooling-of-interests accounting" treatment is generally supported by reasoning that no new basis of accountability is required since the two (or more) companies are continuing operations as one company in a manner similar to that which existed in the past. The presumption is that in effect there has been no purchase or sale of assets, but merely a fusion, merging, or pooling of two formerly separate economic entities into one new economic entity.

By 1960 most business combinations apparently could be accounted for either under the purchase concept or under the pooling concept, and either treatment would be held to be in accordance with generally accepted accounting principles. This situation is one in which confusion is bound to flourish.

At the same time a third possibility of accounting for business combination was suggested by some leading accountants. Under this third method the assets and properties of the acquired enterprise would be accounted for at the fair value of the consideration given, or at the fair value of the properties acquired. Likewise, the assets and properties of the acquiring enterprise would be restated to reflect the value inherent in the combination transaction. While this method was not utilized in practice, and thus was not accorded the stamp of general acceptability, it does merit consideration in a review of the problems of accounting for business combinations.

This third alternative was supported by its proponents on the basis that in essence there has been no acquisition and hence there has been no acquiring company. There has been a pooling of companies, with a new company emerging from the combination that is materially different from any of its individual constituents. Under these circumstances a new basis of accountability should be recognized, so it is asserted, since a new business or economic entity exists. The new entity should have its assets and properties reflected in the records at monetary values most nearly representative of their fair value at the time the entity was born.

The crux of the problem in accounting for business combinations lies in the determination of the value at which the assets and properties newly acquired or controlled should be accounted for in the records of the economic unit resulting from the combination. These assets or properties would be accounted for at different values, depending upon whether the transaction was considered to be a purchase or a pooling of interests. As we will note later, the classification of a combination transaction as a purchase or a pooling of interests for accounting purposes frequently was made arbitrarily and with little relevance to the underlying nature of the transaction.

A Brief Look at Related Issues

The implications of the accounting method selected are numerous. In the purchase method of accounting, the disposition of the difference between the fair value of the consideration given in the combination and the underlying book value of the net assets acquired or controlled becomes an issue. While the difference could go in either direction, generally the fair value has been in excess of book value. The problem of disposing of this difference has a dual impact, once at the initial recording of the transaction, and again at the end of each subsequent accounting period. The difference between the fair value and the book value is usually assigned to specific assets of the company acquired, to specific tangible assets, to goodwill, or to some other specific intangible asset. If portions of this difference are assigned to tangible and intangible assets (other than goodwill), these amounts should be amortized in a systematic manner. If all or part of the difference is assigned initially to goodwill, it should be amortized if it has limited life. Any amortization will, of course, reduce reported income below the amount which would be reported without amortization. (See additional discussion, chapter 4, page 26, and chapter 8, page 87.)

A related problem arises from the income tax implications pertaining to business combinations. Most of the combinations of the late 1950's were "tax-free" at the time of combination. Thus, the tax basis of the property in the hands of the emerging company was the same as the basis in the hands of the preceding company. If the acquiring company used the purchase method of accounting for the assets acquired in a "tax-free" combination, the asset values recorded generally would be different from those existing on the books of the company acquired. Any amortization of this difference for book purposes would not be deductible for income tax purposes. Thus, the use of purchase accounting for "tax-free" business combinations would tend to widen the difference between taxable income and accounting income.

A number of other accounting and reporting problems are also created by business combination transactions. These will be more fully discussed in subsequent portions of this report. At this point it should be emphasized, however, that the effect of the selection of a given accounting method would extend over several accounting periods subsequent to the period in which the combination took place. The effect of the selection of a method of accounting for a business combination would be reflected in the reported income for a series of years, and hence probably in the market values of the stock and in dividend payments. The real significance of the problem of accounting for business combinations lies in these resultant effects.

The Problem Area in Perspective

The accounting treatment afforded the business combination transaction is reflected initially in statements of financial condition (balance sheets). The users of these statements have a right to expect that the dollar amounts contained therein are representative of the assets, properties, and equity interests of the enterprise rendering the report. Under current standards of accounting this does not imply that all the specific dollar amounts appearing within the statement of financial condition are representative of the *current value* of the various items contained in the report. It does imply, however, that the dollar amount initially recorded for any asset, property, or equity interest was representative of the *cost or value* of that item at the date the item became identifiable with that enterprise. The determination of the appropriate dollar amount at which to record the assets, properties, and equity interests over which an enterprise assumes ownership or control by means of a business combination is essential to the presentation of fair, equitable, and understandable financial statements.

Of more significance, however, is the effect which the determination of the appropriate dollar amount has in subsequent accounting periods, as reflected in the earnings statements of the emerging or resultant enterprise. The final figure of reported net profit has significance in the determination of earnings per share, in comparisons with prior periods' net profit, and may materially affect the market price of the stock of the reporting enterprise. Likewise, the final figure of reported net profit may affect bonuses to key employees, contributions to employee profit-sharing plans, declarations of dividends to stockholders, and the effectiveness of stock-option plans.

The management of a corporation has a responsibility to account for those assets and properties entrusted to it by the various equity interests. This accounting should have an objective basis and should be free from any bias favorable to any interest in the enterprise. This responsibility of management is as fully significant in regard to the issuance of shares of stock in exchange for assets and properties as it is in regard to the use of cash or other assets for the same purpose.

Thus, a solution to the problems of accounting for business combinations has significance for many interests. The solution of the problems in this area, as well as those in other troublesome areas of accounting, is the responsibility of the accounting profession. The soundness and equity reflected in the solutions of the profession will not only affect the stature of the profession in the business community, but will also affect many important decisions of those who rely upon the financial reports to provide a basis for their actions.

3

Accounting for Business Combinations Prior to 1949

While the term "pooling of interests" probably did not evolve until later, the two principal accounting characteristics of the "pooling" accounting treatment were recognized as early as the 1920's. These two characteristics involve (1) the carrying forward of the retained earnings (earned surplus) of the constituents as retained earnings of the resultant entity, and (2) the carrying forward of the book values of the assets of the constituents as the book value of the assets of the resultant entity. The following quotation from Wildman and Powell[1] is indicative of the awareness of these issues at an early date.

> A highly controversial point related to consolidations concerns the idea that corporate units lose their surplus when legal consolidation is effected by means of a newly organized successor corporation. Those who contend for this view argue that it is impossible for a new corporation to acquire surplus without having operated a sufficient length of time to have derived surplus from earnings. In other words, a corporation may not begin business with a surplus. Further, they hold that the surplus of a constituent company becomes capitalized when that company becomes consolidated.
>
> The argument just advanced appears to be founded on a view

---

[1] John R. Wildman and Weldon Powell, *Capital Stock Without Par Value*, p. 224. 1928.

that looks to the form rather than to the substance of the matter. Recognition should be given, it seems, to the fact that a new corporation is organized merely as a legal convenience. The value of assets prior to consolidation is not changed necessarily by the legal formality of transferring them to a new owner. The liabilities of constituents are neither increased nor decreased by the process of combination. Under such circumstances it would appear that any excess of assets over liabilities remains the same both before and after consolidation. Finally, if the excess represented surplus available for dividends before consolidation, it must necessarily represent the same thing after consolidation.

The Earned Surplus Question

At this early date it appears that the retained earnings (earned surplus) issue was predominant. Accountants had long had as a general rule the concept that a new corporation could not begin operations with a balance in earned surplus. Or, stated more positively, earned surplus was presumed to have arisen from profitable operations of the entity on whose balance sheet it appeared. Certain combinations effected in the 1920's, however, involved mere changes in form of the entity, without any real change in substance. For example, Company B and Company C, both subsidiaries of Company A, could be consolidated in a new Company D, or they could be merged, with the resultant entity being either Company B or Company C. Under these circumstances it appeared logical to carry forward the combined earned surpluses of the constituent companies to the new entity. This deviation from the general rule that a new corporation should not begin its existence with a balance in earned surplus was apparently well established by 1932.[2]

Consistent with this treatment of earned surplus in such a combination, the assets of the new entity were recorded at those values appearing on the books of the constituent companies. Since the operating aspects of the constituents were unchanged and since the stockholder interests were basically the same, little justification existed for changing the dollar ascriptions attaching to the properties used by the new entity from those existing on the books of the predecessor constituents. The absence of arm's-length dealing in a combination arising from these circumstances would render questionable any new values attached to the assets of the new entity.

---

[2] *Accountants' Handbook,* second edition, W. A. Paton, editor, p. 950. 1932.

Thus, the precedent for a new accounting entity commencing operations with earned surplus and for the use of a predecessor's book values as the basis of accounting for the assets of the new entity was established at a fairly early date. The situations giving rise to the use of these two accounting treatments, however, generally involved mere changes in entity form with an absence of arm's-length bargaining. When combinations were effected, however, by exchanging shares of stock in one company for the shares in a different (and frequently unrelated) company, these previously established practices were extended to apply to the new combinations. By the mid-1940's combinations effected through an exchange of securities were occurring with increasing frequency, and the above accounting treatment of such combinations began to be re-examined.

Gradually a distinction began to emerge between two types of combinations: (1) a combination which was actually a family affair in which a strong degree of affiliation existed between the two companies prior to the combination, and (2) a combination in which the constituents had not previously belonged to the same family and in which any existing relationships were merely those incident to the normal course of business activity. Some began to question the appropriateness of carrying forward earned surplus or of using a predecessor's book value as the accounting basis for combinations of the latter type.[3] The third edition of the *Accountants' Handbook*, published in 1947, had this summary on accounting for business combinations:[4]

> Merger transactions are often effected through an *exchange of securities*. In accounting for such cases the book values of the assets of the one or more companies acquired are often transferred without modification to the accounts of the acquiring company and the aggregate is used as a basis of measuring the stock or other securities issued. This treatment is often questionable. The proper measure of the acquired resources to the acquiring company, and the resulting credit to paid-in capital, is their cost on a cash or equivalent basis. If the securities issued in exchange have a measurable market value such value may well be accepted as a measure of the total cost of the assets taken over. If this approach is not available there remains the possibility of an objective valuation of the property and business acquired.

---

[3] For example, see William W. Werntz, "Corporate consolidations, reorganizations and mergers," *New York Certified Public Accountant*, pp. 379-87. July 1945.

[4] *Accountants' Handbook*, third edition, W. A. Paton, editor, p. 1019. 1943.

... Carrying forward in the accounts of a successor company the amount of earned surplus on the books of a predecessor corporation runs counter to the general rule that the creation of a new corporation should be viewed as the launching of a new enterprise. The new company acquires the assets and affairs of the old concern, not its capital and surplus, and the total consideration becomes paid-in capital. It follows that only in those cases where the operating entity and enterprise-investor relations can be considered to persist throughout the formal changes can the taking of old earned surplus on the books of the new corporation be defended.

"Pooling of Interests"—a New Term Emerges

During the same period a new term, "pooling of interests," began to emerge. One of the earliest uses of this term to describe a type of business combination occurred in hearings before the Federal Power Commission in connection with rate base cases. The term was used to describe certain combinations in which the constituents had previously been so closely related that the existence of arm's-length bargaining was questioned. In these cases the newly emerging entity wished to state its asset values at their fair value at the time of the combination, this value being measured by the value of the securities exchanged in the combination transaction. The Federal Power Commission held that valuation on this basis was improper and that no new values should attach to the properties since no change in substance had occurred. In a 1943 case involving two groups of properties held by different persons, the properties being merged into one company subsequently to be owned jointly, the Commission ruled that:

> ... while it may be tolerable to allow a buyer to capitalize the purchase price he may have paid, ... there is surely nothing to be said in favor of allowing two companies mutually to pool their interests, and from that time forward to treat as vested the values they happened then to have.[5]

In the case cited the emerging company was a new entity. There was, therefore, no suitable basis for valuing its shares. Each of the constituent companies had written up its plant account values prior to the combination and proposed to use the increased values as the basis for the assets of the new company. In a later case, in which

---

[5] *Niagara Falls Power Co.* v. *Federal Power Commission,* July 29, 1943. *137 Federal Reporter,* 2d Series, p. 794. 1943.

the constituent interests had been previously related, the Commission cited the above case and ruled: "It was not a sale by which one party disposed of an interest and another acquired that interest. Just as clearly actual legitimate cost cannot be increased by a transaction which does not result in parting with property."[6]

The term "pooling of interests" was used at this early date to describe a combination *transaction* between various interests in which these interests fused their divergent parts into one enterprise. The term was not used to describe the *accounting treatment* proposed; instead, the accounting treatment flowed from the manner in which the Commission viewed the transaction and its responsibility to maintain reasonable utility rates.

Pooling of Interests—Early AICPA Reference

The earliest use of the term by an arm of the American Institute was in the report of the committee on public utility accounting presented to Council on May 1, 1945. Several propositions concerned with accounting for combinations were included in this report, one of which stated "that no new cost can result from a transaction that ... may be regarded as effecting a pooling of interests."

The committee on accounting procedure considered the report of the committee on public utility accounting and submitted its comments to the executive committee in the form of a letter dated October 20, 1945. This letter contained one of the most complete descriptions of what was meant by a pooling of interests that had been set forth up to that time. A pooling of interests was described as a situation in which two or more interests of comparable size were combined. The term would not properly describe a transaction by which the interests of a small company were combined with those of a company that was substantially larger. This use of the term is of interest in that it sets forth one limiting criterion which the transaction must meet. Presumably two previously unrelated companies of comparable size which combined into one new entity (regardless of the formal method of accomplishment) would classify as a pooling of interests.

While the general proposition in the report of the committee on public utility accounting stated that no new cost can result from a

---

[6] In the matter of The Montana Power Company, United States Power Commission. *Opinions and Decisions of the Federal Power Commission,* vol. 4, Oct. 1, 1943-Dec. 31, 1945, p. 235.

transaction effecting a pooling of interests, the committee on accounting procedure felt that a pooling of interests may represent a situation "in which a new basis of accountability is properly recognized and in which assets are most significantly reflected in the accounting records at monetary values most nearly representative of their fair value at that time.... in the opinion of the committee there is nothing inherent in prior carrying values which in these cases insures or guarantees their usefulness as a basis of accountability for the entity after the pooling of interest."

The position of the committee on accounting procedure cited in the preceding paragraph has never been embodied in the subsequently issued pronouncements of the Institute. The use of fair values in accounting for business combinations will be discussed more fully in chapter 7, page 68.

The committee on accounting procedure of the Institute next turned its attention to the problem of accounting for business combinations in the latter part of the 1940's, during a period when more and more combinations became effected through an exchange of the shares of one company for the assets or shares of another.

Some mergers in this period were described as "poolings of interests," and in some mergers (e.g., Celanese Corporation of America and Tubize Rayon Corporation) such a description of the transaction appeared warranted in view of the concept of this term at that time. Other combinations during this period, however, did not meet even a liberal interpretation of a pooling of interests transaction, yet they were accounted for as if they were (e.g., Caterpillar Tractor Co. & Trackson Co.). In some instances these transactions were labeled "poolings of interests," possibly to lend support to the accounting treatment followed. At any rate, in the late 1940's considerable confusion developed over the term. As will be noted later, the term "pooling of interests," which initially was descriptive of a certain type of business *transaction,* became identified with a series of *accounting entries.* Gradually the relation between the term and the business transaction it described dissolved, and the term became more closely related to an accounting treatment of some combinations.

Accounting Research Bulletin No. 40

Finally, in the latter part of 1950 the committee on accounting procedure of the Institute issued its first official pronouncement dealing with business combinations, *Accounting Research Bulletin No. 40.* The bulletin described those combinations which resulted in a continuance of the former ownership interests as *poolings of interests* and those resulting in new ownership as *purchases*. In addition to this attempt to tie these two descriptive terms to the nature of the transaction involved, the committee indicated the nature of the accounting treatment for each type. The accounting treatment to be followed for a given combination would be presumed to rest upon the nature of the transaction ("the attendant circumstances") and not upon a legal designation of the transaction. There seemed to be little doubt that business combinations were classifiable into two types, that the inherent differences in the two types could be perceived and set forth for all to read, and that once the transaction was classified as either a pooling of interests or a purchase, the accounting for it would be settled.

A "pooling of interests" was described as a combination in which all or substantially all of the equity interests in predecessor corporations continued, as such, in the surviving entity. This continuance would exist when the shares of stock in the surviving entity were received by the owners of the predecessor corporations substantially in proportion to their respective interests in the predecessor company or companies. In addition to the above, a pooling of interest combination would normally involve companies of relatively the same size, would normally result in a continuity of management or the power to control management, and would normally involve companies whose business activities were similar or complementary.

A "purchase" combination was presumed to exist when ownership interests after the combination were not substantially in proportion to those prior to the combination, where the relative size of the constituents was disproportionate, where the combination would not result in continuity of management or the power to control management, and where the constituent companies engaged in dissimilar or uncomplementary activities.

Since no one of these criteria was deemed determinative, one had to conclude that an over-all review of the nature of the combination transaction was essential to arrive at its proper classification. Many combination transactions, however, did not fall into a clear pattern, as far as these criteria were concerned. As a result, a given transaction many times failed to qualify clearly either as a pooling of interests or as a purchase. *Accounting Research Bulletin No. 40* did not provide any guide as to the relative importance of the criteria or as to which of the criteria would be dominant in arriving at the proper classification of the transaction.

4

Accounting for Specific Business Combinations

This chapter presents the results of our study of specific business combinations. In total we reviewed over 350 combinations consummated between 1949 and 1960, and grouped them by the following periods: 1949-1952, 1954-1956, and 1958-1960. The cases which form the basis for the analysis in this chapter were selected on a generally random basis from lists of combinations effected totally or substantially through exchange of shares, the lists being provided by the New York Stock Exchange. All combinations reviewed involved at least one company which was listed on that Exchange. The analysis encompassed review of New York Stock Exchange listing applications pertinent to the stock issuances, review of appropriate prospectuses, review of the accountant's letter in support of the accounting treatment recommended, where those letters were available (mostly for the 1958-1960 period), review of annual reports, and discussions with various public accounting firms.

In each of the three periods selected a number of combinations were effected through an exchange of stock in which the constituent companies were disproportionate in size. These combinations involved two companies, the smaller of which was less than 5% of the size of the larger, whether measured by sales volume, asset values, or the number of shares given to acquire the smaller company. A large number of these combinations were accounted for as purchases. We included only a relatively small number of combinations of this type in the study, since the accounting therefor is fairly well settled, and repetitious review did not appear warranted. Therefore, the statistical information to follow does not reflect accurately the size relationships among the companies actually involved in business combinations. Those combinations involving companies of disproportionate size included in the study and accounted for as purchases were selected because of unusual features in the transaction, because of subsequent changes in the initial accounting treatment, because the acquiring company was involved in other combinations of a greater magnitude during this or a later period, and because the inclusion of a few small combinations was desirable to give the study some degree of completeness.

Combinations Reviewed—Size Relationship

Table 1, below, indicates the size relationship of the constituents involved in the combinations reviewed. This relationship is the number of shares given to the stockholders of the absorbed or acquired corporation, expressed as a percentage of the total number of shares to be outstanding subsequent to the combination.

The table indicates that in general most of the smaller combinations of the first two periods were accounted for as purchases (acquisitions), while the large combinations were accounted for as "poolings of interests." This result is in line with the provisions of *Accounting Research Bulletin No. 40* (issued in 1950) which indicated that combinations involving two companies of disproportionate size would normally indicate a purchase transaction. Chapter 7c of *Accounting Research*

Table 1

Size Relationship of Constituents in Business Combinations

Relative Size of Smaller Company to Surviving Co.	Pooling of Interests 1949–1952	Pooling of Interests 1954–1956	Pooling of Interests 1958–1960	Purchase 1949–1952	Purchase 1954–1956	Purchase 1958–1960
Under 3%	1	1	22	3	7	33
3% – 5%	0	2	15	2	6	11
5% – 10%	5	3	23	26	22	13
10% – 15%	5	6	12	12	7	4
15% – 20%	0	4	10	6	8	2
20% – 30%	9	5	0	5	3	1
Over 30%	6	15	7	0	2	2
Total	26	36	89	54	55	66

Bulletin No. 43 (issued in 1953) contained the same reference to relative size as did *Bulletin No. 40*. Even so, an absolute distinction in accounting treatment based upon relative size is not present. The conclusion appears warranted that during these two periods, relative size was not wholly determinative of the accounting treatment accorded the combination.

Accounting Research Bulletin No. 48 (issued in 1957) modified the relative-size criterion by indicating that a combination involving constituents with as great a size disparity as 90%-10% or 95%-5% could be accounted for as a pooling of interests. Accordingly, as the preceding table indicates, a large number of combinations involving constituents of relatively disproportionate size was accorded the pooling accounting treatment in the 1958-60 period. At the same time, however, the number of combinations treated as poolings during this period in which the smaller company was *less* than 5% of the larger indicates that little attention was paid to the limits recommended in the bulletin. The most disproportionate combination consummated as a pooling of interests to come to our attention was in the ratio of 99.7 to 0.3.

The criterion of size deteriorated because to many it appeared illogical. A question frequently posed was: What is it that permits a 5.1% combination to be considered a pooling of interests and prevents a 4.9% combination from being so considered? The deterioration was gradual, as relatively smaller and smaller combinations gained approval as poolings from the independent accountants and the Securities and Exchange Commission.

The same point is expressed in the independent accountant's letter to the New York Stock Exchange to support a combination with a 99.12% to 0.88% relationship: "... the number of shares of common stock which A ... intends to issue for the business of R ... amounts to less than one per cent (.88%) of ..." shares then to be outstanding. "However, to estop pooling-of-interests accounting for this reason alone would mean that no large company could ever pool with a small one. This does not seem logical." Similar comments were contained in other independent accountants' letters.

Examples of Small Poolings

Two combinations of the earlier periods will illustrate certain aspects of pooling accounting.

The single combination reviewed in the 1949-52 period in which there was an exchange of less than 5% of the stock outstanding in the surviving company and for which the accounting treatment was similar to pooling accounting involved the acquisition of Trackson Co. by Caterpillar Tractor Co. in late 1951. Caterpillar acquired all of the outstanding stock of Trackson (60,000 shares) in exchange for 54,000 shares of its common stock. At the time of the acquisition Caterpillar had 3,764,480 common shares outstanding. In accounting for this acquisition Caterpillar credited its capital account for $540,000, the stated value of the shares issued. In information filed with the Securities and Exchange Commission, Caterpillar proposed to credit the excess ($1,662,000) of the net assets of Trackson Co. at the date of acquisition over the $540,000 either to stated capital or to paid-in surplus. In either event the net assets would be recorded by Caterpillar at book value on Trackson's books. Accounting in this manner for assets acquired is one feature of pooling accounting.

During December 1951 the market value of the Caterpillar stock averaged about $49 per share. Upon this basis the value of the net assets acquired from Trackson would have been $2,646,000. Thus, by pooling the assets at the book value on Trackson's books, the assets were accounted for at $444,000 less than if the transaction had been accounted for as a purchase, with the market value of Caterpillar's shares used as the basis for the entry.

A second feature of pooling accounting, the carrying forward of the earned surplus of the acquired company, was not followed here. Instead, the earned surplus of Trackson would become capital or capital surplus of Caterpillar. As will be noted later, several combinations during this period were accounted for in this manner — the assets were "pooled," while the earned surplus was "purchased."

In the 1954-56 period the greatest size disparity in the pooling combinations we studied existed in the Union Carbide and Carbon Corporation (now Union Carbide Corporation) merger with Visking Corporation in 1956. Union Carbide issued 864,449 shares in exchange for all the properties and assets of Visking, or 2.8% of the shares to be outstanding subsequent to the combination. Union Carbide credited its no-par capital-stock account for the amount in the capital-stock account of Visking ($12,305,791) and credited its earned surplus with the Visking earned surplus ($12,867,308). The book value of the net assets of Visking was $25,173,099, and this amount became merged with the Union Carbide asset values.

As will be developed in the discussion to follow, the combining or merging of the earned surpluses of the constituent companies was much more predominant in poolings in this period than it had been in the 1949-52 period. Apparently the reluctance to add one entity's earned surplus to that of a different entity was overcome to some extent during this period.

The application of the pooling treatment to the Union Carbide-Visking combination resulted in a material difference in the basis of accounting for the assets from that which the purchase treatment would have created. The market value of the shares of stock which Union Carbide gave in the exchange approximated $97 million, or $72 million greater than the amount at which they were accounted for. Without expressing a judgment as to the propriety of the accounting accorded this transaction, we note that one consequence of the use of the pooling treatment was to reduce by $72 million the charges to future income accounts, charges which would otherwise have been made if the $72 million was apportionable to tangible assets or to goodwill subject to amortization.

Accounting for Assets

One of the basic differences between the purchase and the pooling accounting treatments lies in accounting for the assets "acquired" in the combination. In a pooling no assets are deemed to have been "acquired," with the result that the assets of the resultant company are, in effect, merged at the book values on the contituents' books (subject to some minor adjustments). In a purchase the assets of the acquired company usually have a value different from the book values of the vendor. Table 2, page 31, indicates the accounting treatment accorded this difference in the purchase combinations included in our study.

The table discloses several points of interest. First, during the 1949-52 period there was a high degree of direct write-off to earned surplus. A direct write-off to earned surplus has the effect of accounting for the assets or properties received at their previous book value. No attempt is made under this treatment to apportion the excess to specific assets, nor is it carried forward as goodwill. Thus, the direct write-off results in carrying forward asset values on the same basis (book value) as they would have been carried had the combination been recorded as a pooling.

During the 1954-56 period, however, direct write-offs were rare. While Chapter 7c of *Accounting Research Bulletin No. 43* did not indicate any change in attitude of the accounting procedure committee on this point, Chapter 5, dealing with accounting for intangibles, was quite clear in its objection to direct write-off of an excess arising in this manner. In all likelihood the absence of direct write-offs is a reflection of the position taken by the committee on accounting procedure as well as by the similar position of the Securities and Exchange Commission. By the 1958-60 period the policy against direct charge-offs to earned surplus was apparently widely followed. The force of the disapproval by the American Institute of Certified Public Accountants and the Securities and Exchange Commission of this previously common practice proved to be effective. One effect of the absence of direct write-off was to clarify the distinction between a purchase and a pooling in accounting for assets.

A second point of interest is the absence of any trend in the allocation of the excess, where the excess was recorded on the books of the surviving company. In all three periods the excess was allocated to

Table 2

Accounting for Difference Between Cost and Book Value of Assets: Purchase Combinations

	No. of Combinations			Subsequent Amortization		
Difference Accounted for as:	1949–1952	1954–1956	1958–1960	1949–1952	1954–1956	1958–1960
Excess of Cost over Book Value, Charged to:						
Tangible Fixed Assets	12	10	17	9	9	12
Goodwill	7	20	17	1	8	13
Goodwill and Assets	1	8	4	1	6	3
Intangibles Other than Goodwill	0	0	5			3
Depreciation Reserve	1	0	0			
Earned Surplus, Directly	12	1	0			
Capital Surplus, Directly	0	2	0			
Excess of Book Value over Cost, Credited to:						
Goodwill	9	5	3			
Tangible Fixed Assets	1	1	4			
Earned Surplus	1	0	0			
Excess Not Determinable or Insignificant	10	8	16			
Total	54	55	66	11	23	31

tangible assets in a significant number of cases. Throughout the period the excess was assigned to specific tangible assets about as frequently as it was assigned to goodwill. The problem of allocating the excess among specific assets was apparently solved satisfactorily.

A third point is the definite trend toward adoption of a policy of amortization. (It is also possible that amortization was followed in other situations where the data available to us were silent on the point.) The rather substantial increase in the amortization of the excess classified as goodwill appears to reflect the influence of the policy of amortization set forth in Chapter 5, "Intangible Assets," of *Accounting Research Bulletin No. 43.*

While further discussion of the accounting for goodwill, including the Institute's recommendations, will be dealt with in a later chapter, we note the apparent hesitancy in earlier periods to adopt a plan of systematic amortization. Of interest on this point is a quotation from the listing application filed by G. C. Murphy in connection with the acquisition of the Morris 5 & 10 Cent to $1 Stores, Inc. (Oct. 1951). The goodwill, based upon market value of the shares given, was to be $5,500,000, as compared to a net asset book value of $4,870,000 for Morris. The shares transferred to Morris were approximately 10% of the shares then to be outstanding. The listing application had this to say regarding the policy on amortization of goodwill:

> The Corporation has no present intention of charging off all or any part of said excess against Income, Earnings Retained in the Business, or Paid-In Surplus, for the reasons that in the opinion of the Corporation the going concern value of all the Morris Common and Preferred Stock exceeds the recorded value; that no depreciation in such going concern value is foreseeable; and that it is anticipated said value will increase. The Corporation is of the opinion that the charging off, at this time, of all or any part of said excess would reflect an improper recordation of the transaction and that subsequent financial statements of the Corporation would present an improper reflection of the going concern value of Morris.

Accounting for Earned Surplus

In both *Accounting Research Bulletin No. 40* and Chapter 7c of *Accounting Research Bulletin No. 43* the merging of the earned surplus accounts in a pooling combination is permissive. In the 1949-52 period the earned surplus accounts were merged in only 11 of the 26 poolings reviewed. By the 1954-56 period this practice was more widely accepted, and in 27 of the 36 poolings reviewed the earned surplus accounts were fully merged. In addition a portion of the earned surplus of the nonsurviving company was carried forward in eight other cases.

In *Accounting Research Bulletin No. 48* the position of the committee on accounting procedure on the carrying forward of earned surplus in a pooling combination was defined more clearly. The recommendation was made that the earned surplus accounts of the constituents should be merged, except to the extent otherwise required by law or appropriate corporate action.

In the 1958-60 period earned surplus was capitalized in seven of the 89 poolings examined. In at least three of these seven poolings, however the facts clearly indicated that the capitalization of earned surplus was necessary because of legal requirements in the state of incorporation. Ohio, for example, will not permit the carrying forward of earned surplus of a company acquired in a combination unless specific requirements are met to qualify the transaction as a statutory merger. Similar laws exist in several other states.

In two other poolings (both of which were accomplished by a retroactive change in the original accounting treatment, a phenomenon to be discussed in detail in Chapter 5, page 43) earned surplus was capitalized by action of the board of directors. In one of the poolings the accounting for the combination was, in effect, combined with a quasi-reorganization, so that the resultant entity began operations with no earned surplus or deficit. In this case a substantial deficit would have existed had the provisions of *Accounting Research Bulletin No. 48* been followed.

In regard to this aspect of the problem the existence of legal barriers to the carrying forward of earned surplus poses a problem of reconciling conflicting standards. While accounting must operate within a legal framework, adequate disclosure of "surplus available for dividends" in a legal sense can still be achieved in a manner to satisfy legal requirements while at the same time accomplishing what is considered to be appropriate accounting treatment.

Summary—Accounting Aspects

In summary, the accounting for business combinations during the 1949-52 period may be characterized as being confused. Combinations which were accounted for as poolings from the asset side of the picture, that is, in which the assets acquired were recorded at the book values on the books of the acquired company, did not consistently follow the pooling concept as to the stockholders' equity. Furthermore, in numerous poolings in this period the earned surplus of the acquired company was capitalized and became a part of the capital surplus of the surviving company. Logically, a pooling would require the merger of earned surplus accounts of the combining companies, with other stockholders' equity accounts also being combined, except for adjustments necessary to meet legal requirements as to par or stated value of stock issued.

Confusion also existed in accounting for purchase combinations. In the purchase concept of a business combination one company buys or purchases the assets or stock of another, accounting for the acquisition on the basis of the cash or fair value of assets or stock given or the fair value of assets or stock acquired, whichever is more readily determinable. A number of purchases during this period, however, involved direct write-offs of a portion of this cost to earned surplus, the amount generally being equal to the excess of market value of stock issued over the book value of the assets acquired. The net effect of such write-offs is to account for the assets acquired as if the combination were a pooling of interests.

The accounting for business combinations during the 1954-56 period was certainly more clear-cut than in the 1949-52 period. Once the combination was classed as either a purchase or a pooling of interests, the accounting to reflect the transaction fell into one of two well-defined patterns. There was an absence of the capitalization of earned surplus in pooling combinations that was so prevalent in the earlier period. Likewise, there was an absence of the direct write-off to earned surplus of the excess of cost over book value in purchase combinations that was found frequently in the 1949-52 combinations.

Likewise, in the 1958-60 combinations we reviewed, greater consistency existed with regard to the asset side of the problem of accounting for those combinations classed as poolings. *Accounting Research Bulletin No. 48* clearly stated that when a combination was deemed to be a pooling of interests, a new basis of accountability did not arise. Our review indicated that for those combinations deemed to be poolings, the assets of the various constituents were carried forward at the underlying book values on the respective corporate books. Occasional adjustments to the book values were made to conform the accounting practices of the constituent companies to each other or to attain closer uniformity in the accounts. Capitalizations of earned surplus and direct write-offs to earned surplus in purchase combinations were all but absent in this period.

Criteria for Determining the Nature of the Combination

Subsequent to *Accounting Research Bulletin No. 40* the American Institute's committee on accounting procedure attempted to clarify the issues in accounting for business combinations through issuance of Chapter 7c of *Accounting Research Bulletin No. 43* and *Accounting Research Bulletin No. 48*. A brief look at certain changes in this series of bulletins may provide a better understanding of some of the developments in this area between 1949 and 1960.

Accounting Research Bulletin No. 40 stated that the distinction between a pooling of interests and a purchase is to be found in the attendant circumstances. The "attendant circumstances" specified by the committee were continuity of ownership interests, relative size of constituent companies, continuity of management or power to control management, and similarity or complementariness of businesses to be combined.

With respect to relative size, we have already seen that it no longer is used as a basis for distinguishing between a purchase and a pooling. In addition, the basic criterion of *Accounting Research Bulletin No. 40* (continuity of equity interests in a pooling combination) was apparently of little importance in making a clear distinction in those cases where an exchange of shares was involved. While it is true that the vast majority of the combinations effected through share transfer resulted in continuity of equity interests, many combinations effected in this manner were accounted for as purchases rather than as poolings.

Bulletin No. 48 reiterated the various criteria set forth in earlier bulletins, with emphasis again upon a consideration of all the attendant circumstances. Most of the criteria set forth involved matters of degree and (with the exception of relative size) the bulletin did not give any indication of the range of deviation permissible before a combination transaction would fall clearly into one category or the other. Likewise, the bulletin did not indicate any criterion for the existence of a pooling, the absence of which would prevent use of the pooling treatment.

Continuity of Ownership Interests

Probably the most significant single criterion cited in the accounting research bulletins to indicate a pooling of interests was that the holders of substantially all of the ownership interests in the constituent corporations become the owners of a single corporation which owns or controls the assets and businesses of the constituent units.

A literal interpretation of this criterion would indicate that the type or class of equity interest given in the exchange should correspond closely to the type of equity interest disappearing in the combination. Thus, if Company A is to combine with Company B and if Company B has outstanding common stock only, Company A should presumably issue its common shares in exchange for the B stock outstanding. If Company A were to issue preferred shares or a class of common stock with provisions different from its regular common stock, a question would arise as to the continuity of ownership interests.

Such a concept of continuity of ownership interests would also appear to be consistent with a concept of a pooling of interests in a business sense, as distinguished from an accounting sense. Thus, for two companies to merge, or pool their interests, and continue operations as if they had always been one business unit, all ownership or equity interests subsequent to the merger should presumably stand in comparable relationships to one another. This would appear to be the intent of the criterion cited above.

Prior to the 1958-60 period, substantially all poolings met this criterion. While preferred stock was used in some cases, these shares were given in exchange for shares of a similar type in the company disappearing in the combination. In the 1958-60 period, however, preferred stock was used, either in whole or in part, to effect an exchange involving only common stock. While the preferred was at times voting stock, our analysis revealed that the equity interests of the disappearing corporation (or the corporation continuing in a subsidiary relationship) were not, subsequent to the acquisition, substantially identical to the equity interests continuing in the acquiring or parent corporation.

The use of the pooling treatment for combinations in which the equity interests of the constituent corporations were substantially different subsequent to the combination than prior thereto was not prevalent during the 1958-60 period. Sufficient examples existed, however, to indicate that at least in these combinations the criterion of continuing equity interests was not deemed to be essential.

The criterion of the continuance of all pre-existing equity interests as equity interests in the continuing corporation is difficult to evaluate. From the data available it appeared that in substantially all poolings all or a major portion of the equity interests in the acquired or disappearing corporation *intended* to continue as such in the resultant corporation. The very negotiability of shares of stock, however, virtually prevents determination of whether the intent did in fact materialize.

We note that several people questioned the validity of this criterion. The critics contended that the criterion was virtually impossible to evaluate, and that it imposed a requirement on the new shareholders which was not similarly imposed on the old shareholders. The latter could divest themselves of their shares at any time. The question raised was: What should the retention of shares by the newly entering shareholders have to do with the accounting for the combination?

Continuance of Acquired Company as a Subsidiary

In describing a pooling, *Accounting Research Bulletin No. 40* speaks of the surviving corporation without an implication of continued existence for the acquired or absorbed company. In the 1949-52 period, only one combination reviewed, which could be considered as a *pooling*, involved the continuation of the acquired company as a subsidiary. Even in this one instance the case is not clear-cut because the market value of the shares transferred in the exchange approximated the underlying value of the net assets acquired. In ten of the 53 *purchase* combinations, however, the evidence was clear that the acquired company was to remain in existence in a subsidiary relationship following the combination.

A rather sharp change is made in *Accounting Research Bulletin No. 48* in regard to the existence of one or more of the constituents in a subsidiary relationship following consummation of the combination transaction. The bulletin indicates that the continuance in existence of one or more of the constituent corporations in a subsidiary relationship to another of the constituents or to a new corporation does not prevent the combination from being a pooling of interests if no significant minority interest remains outstanding, and if certain other tax, legal, or economic reasons would also support the maintenance of the subsidiary relationship.

Thirty-one of the 89 combinations accorded the pooling treatment in the 1958-60 period gave specific indication that the acquired unit would remain in existence in a subsidiary relationship. An explicit "pooling" would occur as an incident to the preparation of consolidated financial statements.

Classification of Transaction

Our review of the combinations consummated during the 1958-60 period, along with a consideration of the combinations of the earlier periods, leads to the conclusion that the nature of a business combination was lacking in clarity by the end of 1960, both as to the concept itself and as to the practical classification of the various combinations. *Accounting Research Bulletin No. 48* did little, if anything, to clarify the issues in this area. Many people indicated that the actual effect of *Accounting Research Bulletin No. 48* was to permit even wider latitude in determining the treatment of a given combination than had previously existed. Thus, rather than having criteria against which the aspects of a given combination could be evaluated to determine its appropriate accounting treatment, *Accounting Research Bulletin No. 48*, in effect, presented the criteria in such a manner that any given combination could be supported as either a purchase or a pooling, depending largely upon the intentions or desires of the parties to the transaction. (Further discussion will be presented on this aspect of the problem in chapter 7, page 68.)

The Problem of Intangibles

Earlier in the chapter we noted (1) the gradual elimination of the practice of immediately charging off to earned surplus any excess of cost over book value arising in a combination, and (2) a gradual increase in the practice of amortizing this excess, regardless of how it was classified at the initial recording date. The impetus to these changes was provided by Chapter 5 of *Accounting Research Bulletin No. 43*, the chapter dealing with accounting for intangibles.

Chapter 5 of *Accounting Research Bulletin No. 43* (issued in 1953)[1] involved a significant change from a position taken earlier by the committee in *Accounting Research Bulletin No. 24* (issued in 1944).[2] The earlier bulletin recognized the then "accepted practice" of eliminating those intangibles which had an unlimited term of existence by writing them off against any available surplus, but did not feel it necessary to propose a rule prohibiting such disposition, although it did discourage the practice, especially if the charge-off was to be made to capital surplus. *Bulletin No. 43* omitted any discussion on this point, thereby omitting any sanction to an immediate direct charge-off to surplus of intangibles having an unlimited term of existence. Herein lay a basic change in the position of the Institute committee on accounting for intangibles.

In the period subsequent to *Bulletin No. 43* the practice of a direct

---

[1] Reproduced in Appendix, p. 127.
[2] Reproduced in Appendix, p. 115.

charge-off of the excess of cost over book value of a subsidiary's stock was no longer considered to be appropriate accounting. This meant that any excess was to be allocated to tangible or intangible assets where an appropriate basis for an allocation existed, or to be classified as goodwill to be amortized to income beginning either immediately or at some future date when a limited term of usefulness could be ascertained. The principal significance of this new position of the committee was that the excess of cost over book value of a company's stock acquired would henceforth result in charges to income rather than to surplus. The only exception would arise when the amount of the charge-offs would distort the income statement. The position of the committee, as set forth in *Accounting Research Bulletin No. 43*, was accepted by the Securities and Exchange Commission as being appropriate accounting for intangibles.

Our study indicated the likelihood that this new position on accounting for intangibles had a significant influence upon the accounting for business combinations. Since the pooling accounting treatment would not create any excess of cost over book value of assets, pressures developed to employ this treatment. In a period of rising prices such as the 1950's, the pressures to avoid the future charges to income that the purchase treatment involved were almost irresistible. While it is virtually impossible to determine which of many factors are determinative in selecting among alternative accounting treatments, our discussions with a number of leading accountants indicated that the future charges to income which the purchase treatment would create were a significant consideration in the selection of the pooling treatment to account for many combinations. (We consider this aspect of the problem further in chapter 7, page 68.)

Income Tax Influence

Various provisions of the Internal Revenue Code, particularly the 1954 revision, provided particular stimulus to the increase in combinations effected. The tax law identifies six avenues to accomplish a corporate reorganization without incurrence of an immediate tax liability for any of the parties involved. These are:

1. A statutory merger or consolidation. Thus, a business combination effected within the laws of the various states will be tax-free as of the date the combination is effected.

2. An acquisition by one corporation of the stock of another cor-

poration. To be tax-free the acquiring company in the combination can give up *only* voting stock and it must gain control of the company acquired. Control for purposes of this section of the law requires ownership of stock possessing at least 80% of the total voting power and ownership of at least 80% of the total number of shares of all other classes of stock. If the 80% provisions are not complied with, the transaction is not a corporate reorganization for purposes of the tax relief provided by the law.

3. An acquisition by one corporation of the properties of another for stock. The stock given by the acquiring company can be *only* voting stock and the acquiring company must gain control of substantially all properties. If over 80% of the fair value of the properties is acquired in exchange for the stock given, cash or the assumption of liabilities may be present for all or part of the remainder without the transaction being disqualified as a tax-free reorganization.

4. A transfer of assets to another corporation for controlling stock. This covers a reorganization wherein a part of an existing corporation is split-off in some fashion in such a manner that the transferor corporation or its shareholders subsequently control the company to which the assets are transferred. Control is measured as in (2) above.

5. A recapitalization of an existing corporation.

6. A change in name, identity, or form.

Any corporate reorganization falling within the scope of one of these provisions becomes "tax-free." This relief from tax reflects a policy that taxpayers should not be forced to liquidate assets or properties received in an exchange in order to meet tax obligations which would otherwise arise. Any tax which would otherwise fall due is postponed until the time that the securities or properties received in the transaction are disposed of in the normal course of business. To compute the tax due at that future time, the basis of the securities or properties received in the transaction is the same as the basis which the securities or properties given up in the transaction had prior to the transaction.

The postponement of tax has special significance for the seller whose properties have already appreciated in value to a considerable degree and who would therefore be subject to a sizable tax. The seller can lessen his tax by selling the securities or properties received in small lots over a number of years, some of which would likely be retirement years in which other taxable income would be considerably lower than in years prior to retirement.

Of the above six types of corporate reorganizations resulting in a tax-free transaction, the first three have been significant in the business combination movement of recent years, and the second type, involving an exchange of stock for stock, has probably been the most important. While the effect of these provisions of the tax law as a motivating force behind business combinations is difficult to measure, the specific form which a combination has taken, once the decision to combine has been made, appears to have been influenced considerably by these tax-law provisions.

Likewise, it is fairly evident that the accounting for business combinations has been significantly influenced by the tax law. Since the properties acquired in exchange for stock will have the same basis for tax purposes in the hands of the acquiring company as they had for the previous owner, the use of the pooling treatment for tax purposes was encouraged. This treatment for tax purposes would not block the treatment as a purchase on the books, but if the purchase treatment were in fact used for business purposes any excess would have no tax basis. In subsequent years, amortization of this excess for accounting purposes would result in a charge to income, without a related deduction for tax purposes. The increased use of the pooling treatment for combinations effected through the use of stock was no doubt encouraged in large measure by the consistency which such treatment accomplished between the book and the tax basis of the properties.

Summary

Accounting Research Bulletin No. 48 was the third attempt of the committee on accounting procedure to express clearly a concept of a business combination, and, of more significance, to express clearly the distinctions between those combinations which were poolings of interests and those which were purchases. Our review of combinations consummated subsequent to the issuance of *Accounting Research Bulletin No. 48* fails to disclose evidence of improved clarity in the concept of a business combination. In fact, if anything, the distinctions between those combinations deemed to be purchases and those deemed to be poolings were less clear than in previous periods. That is, while the various combinations entered into during the period were classified either as purchases or as poolings, a review of the conditions underlying similar combinations which were classified differently failed to disclose the justification for a difference in classification. Numerous accountants with whom this problem was discussed argued strongly that careful analysis of the criteria to guide appropriate classification as set forth in *Accounting Research Bulletin No. 48* would lead to the conclusion that these criteria as stated were either inappropriate or inadequate bases upon which to distinguish a combination as a purchase or a pooling.

Once a combination was classified as a purchase or a pooling, however, the accounting entries to reflect the transaction took on an increasingly definite pattern in the 1958-60 period. Thus, accountants appeared to have a rather sharply drawn distinction as to the alternative methods to account for business combinations, even though there was not a related, sharply drawn distinction on the way to determine which of these two alternative bases was appropriate for a given combination. Two alternative bases of accounting for business combinations could result in widely divergent asset values and stockholder equity allocations even though a given combination many times appeared as capable of classification as a purchase as it was as a pooling.

5

Disclosure of Business Combinations in Annual Reports

The problem of reporting the significance of business combination transactions exists regardless of the accounting entries used to reflect the transaction. Thus, this chapter will be primarily concerned with the current status of informative disclosures in connection with these transactions and not with their historical development.

For the 1958-60 period 84 combinations were selected for the purpose of tracing through the various aspects of the reporting treatment accorded the combination transaction. Annual reports for the year in which the combination was consummated were reviewed in this analysis. Of these 84 combinations, 52 were accounted for under the pooling-of-interests concept and 32 as purchases.

Disclosure for "Pooled" Combinations

In general the disclosure of those combination transactions accounted for as poolings of interests was adequate. Of the annual reports for 52 "pooled" combinations reviewed, 38 mentioned the pooling in the president's letter, 34 gave it separate or additional mention in the body of the report, and 26 included the combination transaction among the highlights of the year.

Widespread disclosure was also given to the pooling combinations in the notes to the financial statements, and to a lesser degree in the statements themselves. Thus, in 49 of the 52 poolings the combination transaction was either mentioned or discussed in a footnote to the financial statements. While the footnote generally described the nature of the transaction, including disclosure of the number of shares transferred in the exchange, in a few instances the footnote indicated only that a pooling of interests had taken place. Here the presumption apparently was that the reader understood adequately the nature of a pooling of interests.

For example, during 1959 General Telephone & Electronics Corporation entered into business combinations with Sylvania Electric Products Inc. and Lenkurt Electric Co., Inc. Their 1959 annual report included the following note to the financial statements (page 31). This note was the only disclosure of these combinations in the financial statements:

(1) *Principles of Consolidation*

Except for the exclusion of minor subsidiaries, all telephone subsidiaries and all manufacturing subsidiaries in 1959 have been consolidated. Such exclusion had no significant effect upon the consolidated statements. The 1958 financial statements have been restated to include Sylvania Electric Products Inc. and Lenkurt Electric Co., Inc. acquired in 1959 and accounted for on a pooling-of-interests basis.

In 36 of the 52 pooled combinations the financial statements or footnotes provided explanation of the change in retained earnings resulting from the combination. For the other pooled combinations the beginning balance of retained earnings was not changed (the merged company's retained earnings being capitalized) or was merely restated to include the retained earnings of the "new partner" in the corporation. In over one-half of the reports in which the change in retained earnings was disclosed the explanation was accomplished within the body of the statement of retained earnings. In other reports footnote disclosure was used, while both avenues of disclosure were utilized in five of the 36 reports.

Disclosure for "Purchased" Combinations

Combinations accounted for as purchases were also discussed or disclosed in annual reports in many instances. Of the 32 purchase combinations reviewed 17 were discussed in the president's letter, 19 were given separate disclosure in the body of the report, and seven reports mentioned the combination in the highlights for the year. In addition, disclosure in the notes to the financial statements was common, occurring in 14 reports. The excess of cost over the book value of assets acquired was given specific mention in eight reports, with the accounting treatment disclosed in seven of the eight.

An example of relatively full disclosure in an annual report of a purchase combination is found in the National City Lines Inc. report for 1959 (page 7):

> A. *Acquisition of United Motor Express, Inc.,* ...
>
> In late November, 1959, the Company, after approval by its stockholders, acquired all of the outstanding stock of United Motor Express, Inc. in exchange for 74,074 shares of its previously unissued common stock and $6,000,000 in cash. The accounts of United Motor Express, Inc. and its wholly owned subsidiary (Los Angeles-Seattle Motor Express, Inc., a motor freight carrier) have been included in the accompanying consolidated financial statements from December 1, 1959. The excess (approximately $1,600,000) of the purchase price over the detailed appraised value of the underlying net assets of the companies acquired has been included in intangible property and is being amortized over a 25-year period.

Disclosure of Nature of the Transaction

In several instances the footnote disclosure of poolings included a fairly detailed description of the nature of a pooling and of the accounting results flowing from use of the pooling concept. In other reports the terminology used to describe the business combination was not so clear-cut. For example, the footnote disclosure might describe the combination as "a pooling of interests for accounting purposes," while other representations of the transaction in the report would indicate that the resultant company was in fact an acquirer or purchaser of the other constituent during the year. Our previous discussion indicated that the line of distinction between a purchase and a pooling has been quite hazy. The wording of some reports suggests that a given combination transaction was accounted for as a pooling when in fact the participants in the combination may actually have conceived of the transaction as a purchase, a buy-sell transaction. A few examples are presented to illustrate the use of terminology indicating a purchase or acquisition when the transaction was accorded pooling treatment.

> On August 1, 1959, the Aurora Gasoline Company was acquired as a wholly owned subsidiary through the exchange of 874,422 newly issued shares of The Ohio Oil Company's common stock for all the capital stock of the Aurora Gasoline Company. This transaction is reflected through a pooling of interests, and. . . .
>
> Annual Report, The Ohio Oil Company, 1959, p. 7.

Also included in the consolidated financial statements are the accounts of Swindell-Dressler Corporation, which was acquired in September, 1959 by an exchange of 111,103 shares of Pullman Incorporated capital stock for all of the outstanding capital stock of Swindell-Dressler Corporation. This exchange of stock has been deemed a pooling of interests and the assets, liabilities, and earned surplus of Swindell-Dressler Corporation have been carried forward in the accompanying consolidated financial statements....
Annual Report, Pullman Incorporated, 1959, p. 15.

In 1959, the Company acquired the net assets of Suntide Refining Company upon exchanging 525,000 shares of its common stock for the remaining 50.4% stock of Suntide outstanding in the hands of others. The exchange was considered a pooling of interests and the assets, liabilities and earnings of Suntide were carried forward at their book value.
Annual Report, Sunray Mid-Continent Oil Company, 1959, p. 14.

In general, we conclude that many business combination transactions were adequately described in the financial statements. We also note the likelihood that many readers of financial statements are not conversant with the nature of a pooling of interests and that a mere labeling of a given combination as a "pooling of interests" will do little to provide these readers with an understanding of the nature of the transaction consummated.

Operating statements for the year of combination were generally presented on a basis consistent with the concept adopted to account for the combination. To the extent the information could be ascertained, the operating statements for those companies which had a pooling-of-interests combination included the results of operations for the various constituents for the entire year. Similarly, when the combination was accounted for as a purchase, the operating results for the emerging company generally included the operating results of the acquired company for only that portion of the year in which the company was owned. In the latter cases, however, full year amounts for key items were frequently reported in a footnote.

Recasting of Preceding Year Data

Of the 52 pooling combinations reviewed, the financial data for the preceding year were recast in 31 reports to reflect the operations as if the various constituents had been one company throughout the year preceding the year of combination. In addition, similar comparative data were reported in notes for four other combinations. In five additional combinations the prior year statements were presented as previously reported and were also restated, generally being labeled as *pro forma* statements. These statements were designed to provide a basis for comparison with the current year's statement. In all such instances data were also presented for the current year for the "acquiring" company only. The financial statements for the preceding years were not recast for any of the combinations accounted for as purchases.

In some reports a reason was presented for not recasting the prior year amounts in those reports reflecting pooled combinations and in which no revision was made:

> ... Because of the several different fiscal years formerly used by the Injection subsidiaries, the 1958 consolidated accounts have not been restated to reflect the pooling retroactively; such a restatement would not have a material effect on 1958 net earnings.
> Annual Report, Rexall Drug and Chemical Company, 1959, p. 21.

> ... The net income for the year 1958 has not been restated to include the results of operations of the merged companies since the amounts involved are not material.
> Annual Report, Union Tank Car Company, 1959, p. 17.

> The figures bear no comparison with sales and earnings of prior years because the merger on April 21, 1959, created a totally new situation.
> Annual Report, Glen Alden Corporation, 1959, p. 1.

In a number of other annual reports a specific statement was included that the prior year's amounts had not been recast, but no reason was given to explain why.

As noted above, several annual reports were presented to give effect to a combination entered into subsequent to the reporting date. These reports were described as *pro forma* reports, presenting the financial statements as they would have appeared had the combination been consummated prior to the reporting date. One unusual example of this reporting technique was the Bell & Howell Company's annual report for 1959. On January 15, 1960, Bell & Howell effected a merger with Consolidated Electrodynamics Corporation, with Bell & Howell as the surviving corporation. The statement of income and retained income in the annual report for 1959 contained four columns of data. The columns were headed:

1. Combined, year ended December 31, 1959

2. Consolidated Electrodynamics Corp., year ended December 31, 1959

3. Bell & Howell, year ended December 31, 1959

4. Bell & Howell, year ended December 31, 1958

The statement of financial position contained columns for amounts at December 31, 1959, on a combined basis and for Bell & Howell, and at December 31, 1958, for Bell & Howell.

A similar presentation was noted in the 1958 annual report of The May Department Stores to reflect its subsequent merger with The Hecht Co.

Recasting Five- to Ten-Year Summaries

Financial data for a five- to ten-year period, which many companies include in their annual reports, were not as generally adjusted or recast to reflect the mergers as were the data for the preceding year. The annual reports for 44 of the 52 pooling combinations reviewed included financial statistics for a five- to ten-year period. In 32 of these 44 reports these financial statistics included the appropriate amounts for the pooled companies either for the year of pooling alone or for that year plus the next preceding year. For 12 reports the statistical data was recast to provide the comparative data as if the recently merged companies had been one economic unit throughout the period covered. None of the 32 reports reflecting purchase combinations presented a revision of the comparative data.

We found a diversity of opinion in discussing this aspect of the disclosure problem with various accountants. On the one hand some accountants felt that it was essential to adjust the data if they were to have any validity for the purpose for which they were presented. Only by placing the data for the various years on as similar a basis as possible would the results of the analysis be capable of proper interpretation. It was further argued that without the recasting an artificial growth element is injected into the comparative data.

On the other hand some accountants expressed objections to the continuous recasting of financial data. The feeling was expressed that the degree of acceptability of financial data would likely be impaired considerably if data once presented and certified were subsequently revised. The public might be led to question the credibility of the data on which accountants presently express an opinion. Other accountants expressed the view that continuous revision of statistical data was time-consuming and expensive, possibly to a degree greater than the benefits which would flow from its presentation.

If the two corporate parties to a pooling are approximately similar in size, the case for revision of prior years' financial data appears to be quite strong. The distortion which would otherwise result could be material. On the other hand, if the corporations which are parties to a pooling are of widely disproportionate size, the case for revision is not so great. The chances of distortion are considerably reduced as the disproportionality in size of the constituents increases.

Retroactive Change

One of the most unusual aspects of the business combination problem involves the retroactive change of the accounting treatment originally accorded the combination transaction. A number of combinations, generally but not always involving corporations of a disproportionate size, was originally accounted for under the purchase concept, but later the whole transaction was restated to reflect a pooling of interests.

As will be further emphasized in the following chapter, the phenomenon of retroactive change of accounting treatment appears to support a contention that guides to accounting for business combinations were not clearly drawn nor fully comprehended even as late as 1960. If the accounting entries to record a business transaction were logically based and if they properly reflected the transaction consummated, then any change in the original accounting treatment could be supported only on the basis that the original transaction was misinterpreted or that an error existed in the original recording. However, most of the retroactive changes to restate purchase combinations as pooling combinations were supported by the contention that the interpretation of the "accounting principles" in the combination area had changed. The transaction itself had not changed nor had it originally been misinterpreted, but the accounting concept of the transaction had changed, thus necessitating a revision of the original accounting treatment.

Further examination of a few of the combinations which were retroactively changed will illustrate the general procedure. In 1957 American Machine & Foundry Company acquired the W. J. Voit Rubber Corporation and the J. B. Beaird Company, Inc., in exchange for 121,680 and 153,492 shares of common stock respectively. At that date the shares exchanged represented 3.4% and 4.3% of the American

Machine and Foundry (AMF) shares then outstanding. The market value of the shares exchanged exceeded the book value of the underlying assets by approximately $900,000 (29%) and $2,300,000 (80%) respectively. These combinations were each accounted for under the purchase concept, and the above excess of acquisition cost over book value was added to certain tangible assets with the intention of amortizing the excess by charges against earnings.

The 1957 annual report of AMF included the following statement in Note A (p. 26) to the financial statements: "The statement of consolidated income for 1957 includes the operations of The J. B. Beaird Company, Inc., and W. J. Voit Rubber Corporation which were acquired in January 1957. Sales of these companies for 1957 amounted to $31,647,000."

This accounting treatment remained unchanged through 1958, but the 1959 annual report announced that these two acquisitions were now being considered to be poolings of interests and that the original accounting treatment was being modified to reflect the change. Note A (p. 50) to the financial statements in the 1959 annual report of American Machine & Foundry Company included the following statements:

> In January 1957 the Company exchanged shares of its common stock for all of the common shares of W. J. Voit Rubber Corporation and the J. B. Beaird Company, Inc. These transactions were treated as purchases rather than "poolings of interests" under the then current interpretation of generally accepted accounting principles....
>
> In the light of subsequent changes in the interpretation as to generally accepted accounting principles applicable to business combinations, the Board of Directors in 1959, with concurrence of the Company's certified public accountants, approved a retroactive application of the pooling-of-interests principle to the Voit and Beaird transactions with, however, the retention in capital surplus of the earned surplus accounts of the two companies at January 1, 1957 amounting to $5,078,376....

The note went on to describe the effects of the change on previously reported depreciation charges and net income for 1957 and 1958.

An analysis of these combinations in relation to Chapter 7c of *Accounting Research Bulletin No. 43* and *Accounting Research Bulletin No. 48* leads one to conclude that the change in "generally accepted accounting principles" referred to relates to the "relative size" criterion set forth in these bulletins. At the date of consummation of these combinations the "generally accepted" position with regard to size indicated that these combinations were purchases. Even under *Accounting Research Bulletin No. 48* these combinations would fall below the minimum size relationship indicated, but practice subsequent to the issuance of that bulletin virtually ignored the limits set forth. Since these AMF combinations in all likelihood would have been accorded the pooling treatment had they been consummated in 1959, the retroactive change in accounting treatment was deemed appropriate.

A similar situation arose in the acquisition by Aluminum Company of America of Rome Cable Corporation in 1957. In this transaction Alcoa issued 355,226 shares for all the capital stock of Rome in March 1957. These shares were equal to approximately 1.75% of shares of Alcoa then outstanding. The transaction was recorded as a purchase at that date. In December 1959, Alcoa, through its certified public accountants, made application to the New York Stock Exchange to change this accounting treatment retroactively so that the transaction would reflect a pooling of interests. The following paragraphs indicate the nature of the support for the retroactive change as set forth in the letter from Aloca's accountants to the New York Stock Exchange.

The letter indicates that all factors, except two, set forth in *Accounting Research Bulletin No. 48* to support a pooling of interests "clearly indicate that the acquisition should be treated as a pooling of interests." The two are influence on over-all management of each management and relative size. The letter notes that the acquisition was consummated in an unusually short time during which period "detailed plans were not developed for the integration of Rome's operations with Alcoa's during this period and . . . little consideration was given to the influence which Rome's management would have in the over-all enterprise." The relative size relationship of about 1¾% was also noted.

To support the request for change, the letter notes that since acquisition "steps have been taken to integrate the business of Rome and Alcoa." Certain operating conditions are discussed to suggest that normal business operations have flowed from the combination. It indicated that the president of Rome attended meetings of the top management of Alcoa "from time to time." The conclusion is drawn that, "these facts indicate that the management of Rome does have an influence in the over-all management of the enterprise."

As to the problem of relative size the letter states:

> We believe that there can be no logical grounds for saying that a company may properly employ pooling accounting where stock

CHAPTER 5: DISCLOSURE OF BUSINESS COMBINATIONS IN ANNUAL REPORTS

issued to owners of a constituent company is as low as 5% of combined voting stock, but may not do so simply because a somewhat smaller percentage is the case. To insist on the strict adherence to the percentages stated in *ARB No. 48* would mean that a large company could never pool with a small one.

The positions taken in the letter were accepted by the New York Stock Exchange and the accounting for the combination was retroactively changed.

A slightly different situation arose in the combination of Raytheon Company with Sorensen & Company, Incorporated. In July 1959, Raytheon agreed to issue approximately 33,297 shares of common stock and 15,642 shares of 5½ Series (Cumulative) Serial Preferred Stock for the assets and liabilities of Sorensen. Including conversion of the preferred stock, Sorensen stockholders would hold about 1.4% of the Raytheon stock. The listing application filed with the New York Stock Exchange stated that:

> ... for accounting purposes the acquisition of the assets and business of Sorensen will be recorded as a purchase, and the fair value of the Raytheon shares issued will be assigned to such assets of Sorensen as seem appropriate.

Approximately three months later, in October, Raytheon notified the New York Stock Exchange of a change in accounting treatment and proposed that the transaction be handled as a pooling of interests. Likewise, their independent auditors filed a letter with the Exchange supporting the pooling treatment. The letter listed several factors to offset the acknowledged facts that "Raytheon is dominant in the combination from the standpoint of size, and would appear to be dominant in over-all management, ..." These factors were stated as follows:

1. Clearly a community of interest exists insofar as the nature of the two businesses is concerned.

2. No part of Sorensen business is being abandoned or sold.

3. Contribution by Sorensen in the way of personnel and technical skills is a logical addition and complements those in existence.

4. Substantial continuity of proportionate ownership exists; there are no known plans for significant change.

5. Raytheon shares received by Sorensen shareholders are in proportion to their respective interests. Relative voting rights are not

altered even though some of the securities issued had limited or no voting rights.

This request for retroactive accounting treatment of the transaction as a pooling was approved.

An earlier instance of retroactive pooling involved the 1952 acquisition by Food Machinery and Chemical Corporation of Buffalo Electro-Chemical Co. (Becco) for 302,500 of Food Machinery common stock. These shares represented 10.5% of the shares then outstanding. The combination was accounted for as a purchase, and an intangible asset of $8,232,288 resulted, being the excess of the fair value of the shares given over the book value of the net assets acquired.

In 1957 Food Machinery retroactively changed the original accounting treatment so that the combination was recorded as a pooling of interests. The following statement was included in the listing application to support the change in treatment:

> In January 1957 the American Institute of Accountants revised and clarified its previous bulletin on this subject and the accounts have now been retroactively adjusted to reflect this transaction as a pooling of interests in accordance with the present bulletin and with the concurrence of the Securities and Exchange Commission. . . .
>
> In view of the fact that the equity interest of Becco continues as such in the Company (Food), that the management of Becco is being continued in the company, and that the activities of Becco are similar to certain principal activities of the Company, the Company, by resolution adopted by the Board of Directors on February 28, 1957, and upon consultation with its independent public accountants, has deemed the accounting treatment for a pooling of interests to be appropriate.

Reporting Requirements Under
Accounting Research Bulletin No. 48

Accounting Research Bulletin No. 48 provides only a broad guide as to the nature of appropriate disclosures for combinations in general, although one paragraph (12) discusses disclosures for combinations considered to be poolings of interests. No mention is made of the disclosure for combinations treated as purchases. One is led to conclude that a pooling of interests is sufficiently different from a purchase so that more complete disclosure is required.

One important aspect of disclosure relates to the presentation of operating results for the period in which the combination occurs. Under the pooling of interests concept, two (or more) formerly separate companies combine their assets and properties and merge and continue operations on a basis which suggests that they are and have been one company. A consistent extension of such a concept to a report of operating results for the period of combination would result in a merging or combining of the operating results of the constituent companies into one operating report. The resultant report of operations would be virtually identical to that which would have resulted if the constituent companies had, in fact, been one entity throughout the operating period.

An additional logical extension of the general concept of business combinations would produce a different conclusion as regards a purchase combination. In a purchase one company is acquiring the assets or stock of another, generally with the view of operating the company in the future. In such a transaction one would expect the results of operations for the period of the combination to include the acquiring company's operating results for the entire period but to limit the inclusion of the acquired company's operating results to the portion of the period subsequent to acquisition. While *Accounting Research Bulletin No. 48* does not make reference to this point, such a procedure was followed for virtually all purchase combinations.

Another aspect of disclosure concerns the presentation of comparative data in such a manner that the data are in fact comparative. Thus, if for the year in which a combination takes place the operating data include the results of both constituents on a basis similar to that which would have resulted if they had been one entity for the entire period, it would appear logical that prior period operating data should be modified from that originally presented in order to include the operating data of the newly merged "partner" for the earlier periods. A failure to adjust previously reported data may result in the presentation of data as if they were properly comparative when in fact they are not. Misleading interpretations as to the company's growth could result.

Summary

Even though *Accounting Research Bulletin No. 48* does not establish clearly the guides to follow in disclosing the effects of business combinations in financial statements, reasonable attempts at disclosure are common, particularly if the combination is accounted for as a pooling of interests. Our discussions and research activities indicated that the general concept of the nature of a pooling of interests is not well understood by many people who read financial reports. The confusion in terminology, cited earlier, may have contributed to the relative slowness in grasping the nature of the pooling concept.

When a combination resulted in a "pooling-of-interests" accounting treatment, it was common practice to restate the financial data for the year preceding the year of combination in order to achieve a more accurate degree of comparability. The practice of recasting five- to ten-year financial data was not so well established.

One practice which increased the confusion in this area was the retroactive change in accounting treatment accorded some combinations. The fact of a retroactive change was generally fully disclosed. It is likely, however, that many readers of financial statements failed to grasp the significance of the change or to understand the reasons adduced in its support.

6

The Present Dilemma

While our study was not limited to nor even particularly aimed at a study of the pooling-of-interests concept, this concept dominates the combination area so much as to warrant further consideration at this point.

The Pooling-of-Interests Concept

Originally a pooling of interests involved the concept of a business combination between two or more interests of comparable size. The idea appeared to be that these interests would get together, decide to pool their resources, and from that point forward operate as one business unit. Coincident with this concept an accounting pattern developed to translate the facts of a pooling-of-interests business combination into the language of accounting. This pattern included the carrying forward of asset values as they existed on the books of the constituent companies, without regard to the exchange-price of the consideration involved in the combination transaction. Likewise, the earned surpluses of the constituents could be carried forward as the earned surplus of the surviving company, even though accountants had previously objected to this practice in many combination situations.

Unfortunately, the term "pooling of interests," initially used to describe a type of business combination, was incorporated into technical accounting terminology to describe a method of accounting. Since the practicing accountants were the ones using this term with the greatest frequency, the term soon came to be more closely identified with the accounting procedures which it encompassed than with the type of business combination it purported to describe. By 1960 it was evident that if the accountants would approve the accounting for a given combination as falling within the pooling framework, then the actual combination itself became described as a pooling of interests. Thus, the term "pooling of interests" had come a half circle and in so doing had changed considerably in content from its earlier usage.

Some suggest that the accounting pattern developed to account for "poolings of interests" was not the proper treatment to accord such a transaction. If two or more interests of comparable size joined together, the resulting unit was considerably different from either pre-existing unit. It would be roughly twice as large, control roughly twice as many resources, etc. The management problems would likely be somewhat different, possibly materially so, in the resultant company. Under these circumstances, nothing inherent in prior carrying values insures or guarantees their usefulness as a basis of accountability for the resulting entity. Furthermore, since the resultant entity is materially different from the previous entities, a *new* basis of accountability is required.

Certain features of the position described above have merit. While further consideration will be given to it in the following chapter, we note here that the nature of a pooling of interests is difficult to describe. Even once reasonably well defined, a conclusion as to the appropriate accounting is not necessarily revealed clearly. This suggests the possibility that the development of a concept of a pooling of interests may not hold the clue to the accounting for such a phenomenon.

Forces Acting to Promote Use of the Pooling Treatment

Various forces or pressures existed in the 1950's to increase the use of the "pooling-of-interests accounting" technique in combination transactions. In this period the forces acting to produce a given type of business transaction and those acting to promote a specific type of accounting treatment for the transaction were closely interrelated.

Income tax considerations are clearly influential on both the buying and selling sides of a potential business combination. The tax law provisions which permitted certain business combinations to be effected without incurrence of any tax liability (at the time of the combination) favored the consummation of some combinations. We do not intend to imply here that the "tax-free" exchange provisions of the Internal Revenue Code were designed to stimulate the combination of business corporations. Rather, these provisions in all likelihood were principally aimed at deferring any tax on an exchange of shares of stock for other shares of stock.

Considered in conjunction with rising price levels, a booming American economy, and a generally strong and rising stock market, the influence of the tax law becomes apparent. Potential vendors are far more inclined to sell their businesses for shares of stock than for cash, since the latter would result in an immediate tax liability. To the vendee (the purchaser) the assets acquired have a low basis, which means lower depreciation in the tax return than if the assets had been acquired for cash at current values. The lower depreciation charge will result in higher taxes than if the assets had been purchased for cash. While the payment of more taxes is somewhat of a deterrent to effecting the transaction in a "tax-free" manner, it has apparently been more than offset by the opportunity (a) to conserve cash and (b) to report higher net profits. Higher reported net profits mean, possibly, higher dividends, increasing market prices of the company's shares, higher evaluation of managerial performance, and higher distributions under profit-sharing plans.

The spread between the book value of the assets of the vendor and their going-concern market value as evidenced by the exchange transaction was generally significant in most combinations. If, however, the properties over which the vendee gained control in a "tax-free" transaction were actually recorded at their current values, the excess over the book value on the vendor's books had no status for tax purposes. As a consequence, this current value was not commonly recorded. Instead, the properties were recorded at their book values on the vendor's books, an essential characteristic of pooling accounting. These values were also equal to the tax basis of the properties in a "tax-free" transaction.

The Significance of Accounting for Goodwill

The reasons for the growing acceptance of the pooling concept become even more apparent when other features of its use are considered along with the tax aspects. The most important motivation for use of the pooling accounting treatment in the view of most accountants with whom we discussed the problem concerned the matter of goodwill.

Accounting Research Bulletin No. 43 revised two features of the accepted accounting for intangibles. First, the immediate write-off of intangibles by charges against earned surplus was opposed. Second, the adoption of an amortization policy with respect to goodwill was encouraged. While amortization of all intangibles was not made obligatory, the bulletin favored systematic amortization as soon as any limitation on useful life became apparent.

The opposition to immediate write-off was significant because it acted to prevent a practice which had developed in the late 1940's in accounting for business combinations. A number of combinations in the 1949-52 period were ostensibly accounted for as purchases, with the assets acquired being recorded at the fair value of the assets given in exchange. Immediately after recording the combination transaction, however, any excess of the cost recorded over the underlying book value of the assets acquired was charged off to surplus. The net effect of these entries was, as far as the asset side was concerned, to account for the assets of the acquired or disappearing company in the combination at the underlying book value of those assets. This resulted, of course, in the same asset values as if the pooling concept had been used. Since this procedure for handling the "goodwill" arising in a "purchase" combination was no longer considered generally acceptable after 1953, the combination transaction had to be accounted for as a pooling in order for any excess of cost over underlying book value to be, in effect, eliminated from accountability.

The encouragement of systematic amortization may have had an even greater effect on the increasing utilization of the pooling concept. In view of the inflation during the late 1940's and in the decade of the 1950's, a combination effected through an exchange of shares in the 1950's would normally involve an excess of fair market value of the shares given over the underlying book value of the shares or assets acquired in the exchange. If this excess were to be recorded it would appear either as goodwill or as a part of some tangible asset. In either instance the position of Chapter 5 of *Accounting Research Bulletin No. 43* would encourage the systematic amortization of this excess. Likewise, the policy of the Securities and Exchange Commission throughout this period was to encourage amortization. In fact, a number of accountants indicated to us that the Securities and Exchange Commission's policy on amortization of goodwill had a noticeable effect in reducing or eliminating many goodwill items previously existing on corporate balance sheets. As a consequence the Securities and Exchange Commission was not receptive to the creation of new goodwill items unless an acceptable alternative did not exist.

The amortization of any excess of fair value (cost) over underlying book value would result in a charge against income. In a "tax-free" combination such a charge would not be a deductible item for tax purposes. The amortization would, therefore, reduce net profit, by an increase of expense, but would not decrease the amount of tax payable. As a result, amortization of this type had a double impact, so to speak. Managements in general were not interested in methods or procedures which would depress reported profits or earnings per share; accordingly, they would not favor an accounting procedure that would result in the recording of an "excess," goodwill (or tangible assets), in a "tax-free" business combination.

During this period the emphasis on growth had become extremely great; the existence of stock option plans, profit-sharing plans, and other means of deferred compensation lent added impetus to the desire for higher reported earnings. One problem for a management interested in growth, then, was to find a means to accomplish a business combination transaction and to account for it in a manner that would not be detrimental to earnings.

The fact that a tax-free transaction could be made encouraged growth via the business combination route. The fact that the use of a fair-value basis to record the properties acquired (purchase accounting) would have undesirable effects on reported earnings encouraged the use of book value (pooling accounting) or, as some have bluntly stated, tax basis. While we cannot determine whether the accounting determination or the description of the combination transaction came first, the desire to obtain the accounting results of the pooling-of-interests treatment in all likelihood dictated the classification or description of a number of business combinations.

The distinction is an important one. When classified as a "pooling of interests," a business combination is not faced with the problem of amortizing goodwill. When classified as a "purchase," the surviving corporation is frequently required to record such goodwill on its balance sheet. Then, since this goodwill must be amortized by charges to income annually, *after* taxes, the reduction in net income is often significant. The market value of the surviving company's securities may be affected materially as a result of this reported diminution of earning power. Too adverse a foreseeable impact on earnings may require abandonment of the proposed combination.[1]

---

[1] Homer Kripke, "A Good Look at Goodwill in Corporate Acquisitions," *Banking Law Journal*, Dec. 1961, pp. 1028-29.

Changing Pattern of Pooling Concept

By the late 1950's, the various criteria originally proposed as a basis for classifying a combination transaction as a pooling of interests had been modified in varying degrees from earlier statements of these criteria. However, of at least as great significance is the change in over-all philosophy in applying these criteria. In the early 1950's the general approach seemed to be that for a combination to qualify as a pooling of interests, and to be accounted for in that manner, all of the various criteria should be present. While the accounting procedures for recording business combinations were not so clear during this period, we found relatively few instances of combinations described improperly as poolings of interests in the light of all the attendant circumstances. By the late 1950's, however, we found numerous examples of business combinations described as poolings of interests when one or more of the criteria set forth in *Accounting Research Bulletin No. 48* were admittedly not present.

Thus, by the late 1950's, the approach to the analysis of a combination transaction appeared to be that the *absence* of a given criterion should not *prevent* the transaction from being a pooling of interests if other features suggested that the treatment was appropriate. This approach appears to involve a rather basic change in philosophy from that prevailing earlier. The change is significant in that the later approach involves the application of "negative" reasoning to support the classification given to a particular transaction. We found, for example, this type of reasoning: "Even though Company B's assets and net income are relatively small in relation to Company A (being, say, 2% in each instance) this fact should not prevent the use of the pooling treatment." Or, "even though the common shareholders of Company B received convertible debenture bonds of Company A in exchange for their shares of stock, this fact should not prevent use of the pooling treatment since other requisite conditions were present."[2]

The particular problem posed by this shift in philosophy or concept of a pooling of interests lay in the lack of clarity of meaning which

---

[2] In the October 1960 issue of the *Arthur Young Journal* an article by Frank T. Weston, "Recent Developments in Accounting Practice," pp. 1-4, contains examples of this philosophy. Such features in the combination transaction as preferred stock, "put" options, contingent share arrangements, and size disproportionality are cited as examples of features whose existence should not prevent use of the pooling treatment provided other requisites of a pooling concept exist in a given instance.

developed in the 1950's in regard to "pooling of interests." Accountants then had and still have a relatively definite procedure to apply to a combination transaction bearing the "pooling" label. On the other hand, the "pooling" label became attached to such a diversity of transactions that the end result of the actions taken was to apply the same accounting techniques to business events that were in reality diverse in their business characteristics. The various real pressures which business management felt inclined to exert to gain use of the pooling technique merely added to the lack of clarity. A deviation from a previously accepted position would gain some measure of acceptance. In short order the deviation was being cited as a precedent for an even wider deviation.

Goodwill

"Goodwill" is commonly used as the term to describe the difference between fair value of assets (or stock) given in an exchange and book value of assets (or stock) acquired.

The "goodwill" problem may be broken down into the following elements: (1) its nature, (2) the allocation problem, (3) the amortization problem. Goodwill is often described as an amount paid to acquire an earning capacity in excess of that indicated by the earning capacity of the tangible assets acquired. This excess may arise from any of a variety of circumstances, such as a favorable location, a particularly astute management, a good clientele, or a number of other intangible aspects existing in a particular situation. When the use of the term is limited to this sense, the propriety of reflecting the cost of this intangible in the accounting records is apparent. Likewise, when a payment is made for goodwill identifiable with some specific aspect of that which is acquired, a basis is frequently, if not commonly, in existence for charging off or amortizing this cost to future income periods.

However, the fact is that the term "goodwill" is not generally restricted in usage to this narrow sense. The term is commonly used to describe the excess of cost over book value of assets acquired, or an amount arising in the consolidation process between a parent and subsidiary company, as well as other amounts which many times might more accurately be described by a term other than goodwill. When the use of the term is extended beyond its narrow sense the difficulties of a logical allocation of the amount to future income periods is increased. This difficulty arises principally because a term with a legitimate specific meaning is used to describe an aspect of a business transaction for which it was not intended. If a term is used in an illogical manner, it is understandable that subsequent reasoning flowing from the improper use could create additional problems in logical analysis. The nature of the term "goodwill" today is not clearly defined. This lack of clarity contributes to difficulties in arriving at logical conclusions as to the ultimate disposition of amounts so described.

When the term "goodwill" is used as a catch-all phrase to describe the entire excess of cost over book value of assets acquired, without regard to the nature of the excess, a problem of allocation may arise whether it is recognized as such or not. The generally accepted accounting practice of accounting for assets at cost involves the use of fair value of that which is given in exchange or the fair value of that which is acquired, whichever is more readily determinable, as the appropriate measure of cost. Nothing in this concept requires that the excess of cost (as so measured) of properties acquired over the book value thereof be labeled or described as goodwill. In all cases, this excess should be allocated according to the factor or factors which created it. Accordingly, the excess may be allocated among a variety of accounts, e.g., inventories, fixed properties, intangibles other than goodwill, and goodwill (in the pure sense).

Several accountants told us that the excess which would arise in some business combination transactions could not be allocated on a reasonable basis to any accounts other than goodwill. However, our study of those combinations which were accounted for as purchases disclosed that an assignment of this excess to tangible fixed assets was made very frequently. For example, in the purchase combinations of the 1958-60 period that we studied, an allocation of the excess of cost over book value of assets acquired to tangible assets was made as frequently as the excess was allocated to goodwill. Thus, the problem of allocating the excess to appropriate assets is not insurmountable.

If a basis for allocation of the excess exists, it will generally be evident from an analysis of the combination transaction itself. These transactions often result from arm's-length bargaining between two management or stockholder groups, frequently only after a considerable period of negotiation. When agreement on a combination plan is reached, the terms of the agreement are commonly stated explicitly. Likewise, the various factors which were significant in arriving at the final terms are known to both parties. When the final price is determined (either in number of shares or in dollars) the acquiring company has knowledge of what the combination is to cost them. Likewise, they have knowledge of what they are paying for, what they are acquiring. If the price paid to effect the combination is in excess of the underlying book value of the assets acquired, the officials of the buying company know why they pay the excess. In most combinations the data available from the combination negotiations and from the terms of the final settlement will provide a fair basis for allocating the excess paid.

Another phase of the goodwill problem involves the amortization of the charge after it is recorded. While neither the accounting profession nor the Securities Exchange Commission has, at the present time, a specific requirement for goodwill amortization, the fact remains that most company managements are hesitant to carry forward large amounts of goodwill on the balance sheet. The position of the committee on accounting procedure (Chapter 5 of *Accounting Research Bulletin No. 43*) is essentially that the cost of any intangible should be amortized whenever its period of useful life is determinable or should be charged off in total if it is apparent that no value exists to support the asset.

Two points are of significance. One is the general "climate" in this country which is antagonistic to any showing of goodwill, so labeled, and regardless of the manner in which it arose. The other is the fact that if a business combination is "tax-free" the amortization of any excess that might be recorded, regardless of what it is called, is not deductible for tax purposes in subsequent operating periods. An amortization charge of this type reduces reported earnings, but does not reduce income taxes in any period.

For these reasons the goodwill problem posed some serious obstacles to a more extensive classification of business combinations as purchases rather than as poolings. Since the pooling treatment avoids the goodwill problem, this alternative classification gained wider acceptance than might otherwise have been the case.

Retained Earnings (Earned Surplus)

Another problem area which exists as the result of wide application of the pooling concept involves accounting for retained earnings (earned surplus). The general rule is that when one company acquires another company, the earned surplus of the latter company does not become a part of the earned surplus of the resultant entity. In a business combination which is clearly an acquisition or a purchase, none of the earned surplus of the acquired company is carried forward as earned surplus of the acquiring company. In a "pooling," however, the earned surplus accounts of the companies are combined on the resultant balance sheet, except to the extent that adjustments to the account may be necessary in the combination process.

This apparent deviation is generally supported by the argument that to combine the earned surplus accounts in a "pooling" is not a deviation at all. Under the concept of a pooling an acquisition does not result. Since there is no acquisition, the rule against the carrying forward of surplus is inapplicable.

Some also point out that in a pooling the shareholders in the resultant entity (which would be the combined shareholders of the two previous entities) should not have their earned surplus reduced because of the combination. Such an argument also rests on the contention that in a pooling combination nothing of substance has really changed. The question frequently posed is: Why should the shareholders in the absorbed company, who are now shareholders in the resultant company, have their previous earned surplus eliminated and thereby have their dividend potential diminished?

The matter of surplus availability for dividends is, however, a legal question. In a number of states (e.g., Illinois, Ohio, California) certain legal requirements must be met before the earned surplus of the nonsurviving company in a merger can be carried forward to the surviving company. For example, in Illinois if the assets or capital stock of another corporation are acquired for original-issue stock, the law requires that the board of directors of the surviving company make a determination of the fair value of the assets or stock received as consideration for the stock issued. Thus, when original-issue stock is used in Illinois, the pooling concept, at least from the earned surplus aspect, cannot be followed. If previously issued and reacquired stock (treasury stock) is used to effect the combination, there is no legal requirement, however, that the assets or stock be valued at fair value.

In chapter 4, page 26, we noted that certain combinations were accounted for as poolings from an asset point of view but that the earned surplus of the absorbed company was not carried forward. At that time it was noted that the particular state law involved prohibited the carrying forward of earned surplus in the given transaction. Thus, the end result from an accounting viewpoint was a hybrid treatment.

At the present time the treatment of the earned surplus in those combinations in which the applicable state law does not permit the combined earned surplus accounts to be available for dividends is unsettled. Some accountants contend that while the pooling of interests is an accounting concept rather than a legal concept, it should not violate the applicable state laws. Others contend that the earned surpluses may be combined even if the state law does not permit this, with the surplus available for dividends being shown parenthetically or disclosed in some other manner in the financial statements. The question raised by the shareholders of the absorbed company regarding the loss of their earned surplus in the combination transaction is of little consequence if the state law does not permit the surplus to be available for dividends in the particular combination.

An even more basic question may be raised in connection with the legal requirements cited above. If the carrying forward of earned surplus is an essential feature of a pooling of interests, and if the applicable state law does not permit the surplus to be carried forward, can the transaction qualify as a pooling of interests? This question recognizes that the pooling concept is an accounting rather than a legal concept, and also recognizes the conflict that exists here (as well as in other areas of accounting) between legal and accounting concepts.

Certainly the problem of appropriate accounting for surplus must be resolved both from the accounting viewpoint and from the legal viewpoint if proper accounting for business combinations is to be determined.

Retroactive Poolings

One of the problems which has increased in significance in recent years is the "retroactive pooling" which involves a reclassification of a combination initially recorded as a purchase. The retroactive treatment arises from the changing concept of the nature of a pooling of interests. Thus, for example, Company A and Company B may have joined together in a combination with all the essential attributes of a pooling of interests, except for a disparity in relative size. Assume that in the exchange Company B's shareholders received about 3% of the shares outstanding in the entity subsequent to the combination transaction. At the time of the combination poolings of interests were considered to arise only when the absorbed company received at least 5% of the shares subsequently outstanding. However, if within the next few years several combinations involving only 3% relationships were considered to be poolings of interests, Company A may assert that its combination with B was in fact a pooling of interests within the scope of the term as now defined. Company A may then go back and restate

CHAPTER 6: RETROACTIVE POOLINGS

the transaction as a pooling of interests. (See examples in chapter 5, page 43.

This change in the original accounting treatment of a given transaction is confusing to those interested in the financial data of the company. The question might logically be raised, how can a transaction consummated in good faith and accounted for accordingly be changed subsequently by events not incident to the specific transaction? Is there any logical justification in permitting retroactive changes of this type?

While the problem of retroactive change is not peculiar to the business combination area, it has seen rather frequent application in this area in recent years. The inherent logic of the situation would argue strongly against such a change in the absence of a strong showing of improper accounting in the initial instance.

7

Accounting for Business Combinations— Toward a Solution

Several questions may be posed as a means toward the development of a sound and logical approach to the analysis of the combination problem:

1. What is the nature of a business combination?

2. In what respects are business combinations similar to (different from) other kinds of actions which concern accountants?

3. What guidelines exist within the accounting framework which might suggest possible bases for accounting treatment in this area?

Accounting deals with economic activity, mainly in the form of business transactions. Until a transaction occurs, accountants generally find it difficult to reflect the effects of economic activity. In broad terms a business transaction may be said to involve an exchange of properties and/or equities between two or more independent parties. While business transactions may take many forms, the exchange feature of the transaction is generally crucial for accountants.

Furthermore, economic activity is carried on through specific units or entities, with agents of the unit or entity, generally referred to as management, acting as the lifeblood of the otherwise inert entity. The results of the accounting process are expressed in terms of those units or entities. Most of the time the identification of the entity involved in a transaction is relatively clear-cut. Economic and legal entities frequently coincide. As we will note later in this chapter, identification of the entity of accountability in a combination transaction is a crucial problem.

Thus, we find existing here a three-pronged relationship — an entity through which economic activity takes place; a management, which makes the entity operative; and accounting, which reflects the results of an entity's economic activity. Accounting is concerned with enterprise experience, experience in the form of transactions and their consequences, experience consummated and to be reflected in a systematic manner and expressed in quantitative terms. It therefore serves as a connecting link between enterprise actions in the past and management's decisions for the future.

The Nature of a Business Combination

In looking for the nature of a business combination we must recognize that it can take many forms. But, regardless of the form, a business combination occurs when one company acquires, assumes, or otherwise gains control over the assets or properties of another company by an exchange of assets or equities, or when two companies of equal size merge to form a new enterprise. Thus a business combination is essentially a particular type of business transaction.

As noted throughout this report, two distinct accounting treatments have developed to give expression to business combinations. In the attempt to support each of these two alternatives several contentions have been made. Many of these contentions are concerned with the nature of the transaction. For example, we hear that the business combination is an exchange; that it is not an exchange; that relative economic interests of the constituents have been altered; that they have not been altered.

A thorough consideration of the basic nature of the combination transaction is essential to our study. Accounting must reflect properly the results of economic events relevant to the particular entity, and these results must reflect the basic nature of the action that has transpired if the results are to have validity. Accounting entries which are based on a denial of the substance of a recognized economic event are likely to produce results which are illogical and not representative of the event.

In considering the nature of a business combination, stripped of its accounting considerations, we feel that the conclusion is valid that it is an economic event of some import. Considerable evidence exists to support this conclusion. Certainly the controversy in the accounting profession regarding this phenomenon is indicative that the transaction has importance. Likewise, the considerable negotiations that precede eventual consummation of any business combination support this conclusion. The conclusion seems even more self-evident when one recognizes the importance attached by management to many of these combination transactions when they are described in annual reports to shareholders. These reports frequently contain the assertion that the combination was one of the most significant events of the year.

Our studies lead us to conclude that a business combination is an event of substance and significance. Furthermore, the event is basically an exchange event, one in which two independent economic interests bargain to the consummation of an exchange of assets and/or equities. The discussion which follows is based to a significant extent on the conclusion that a business combination is an economic event of substance, an event involving an exchange of economic interests.

Peculiarities of Business Combinations

This brings us to the second question posed earlier in this chapter: In what respects are business combinations similar to (different from) other kinds of actions which concern accountants?

Any exchange transaction involves the problems of quantification and classification of both the assets or equities received and the assets or equities disposed of or severed. In this light, business combinations are not greatly different from a wide range of other business events. And, such a conclusion is particularly warranted and also universally acknowledged when the combination is consummated through the use of assets to acquire assets or shares of stock.

When the combination is effected through the use of equity elements to gain control over the new assets, however, the exchange transaction involves apparently different elements. The problems of quantification and classification are still those which must be faced, but their solution is not so readily apparent as in those exchanges in which assets are conveyed to effect the exchange.

Some contend that a combination effected through an exchange of capital stock is fundamentally different from a combination effected through an exchange of assets. In an exchange of assets there is little question that an exchange has taken place. The entity has new assets in place of the assets given in exchange. The new assets are commonly accounted for on the basis of the assets, or consideration, given up to acquire them. The end result is a change in the composition of the resources, while total economic resources under the entity's control is basically unchanged.

In a combination involving an exchange of capital stock, however, the entity resulting from the transaction controls the assets previously controlled by the two separate entities. The exchange, if indeed an exchange has taken place, involves the transfer of previously unissued capital stock or of treasury shares of one entity in exchange for the assets (or stock through which the assets will be controlled) of a second entity. Since the capital stock transferred has no basis of accountability on the books of the transferor, this stock does not provide as objective a basis of accountability for the assets obtained as do the assets transferred in an exchange of assets for assets.

We feel that it is precisely at this point that the views of those supporting "purchase" accounting and the views of those supporting "pooling" accounting become divergent. Therefore, a thorough understanding of the points at issue is necessary if one is to be able to arrive at a reasoned conclusion on the proper accounting applicable in the problem area.

Those who favor purchase accounting for a combination effected through an exchange of capital stock are convinced that an exchange transaction has taken place, and that this exchange transaction is basically similar to the wide variety of other exchange transactions in which an entity engages. Particular emphasis is placed (1) on the fact that the assets acquired have entered a new accounting entity (which is also a different legal entity), an entity which formerly had no direct financial interest in the assets, and (2) on the conclusion that the unissued shares of stock used to effect the exchange were mere substitutes for cash, other assets, notes, or bonds. The conclusion, then, is that an exchange transaction has occurred for which the entity is accountable, and that the *manner* in which it was effected should not determine the accounting for it. The exchange should be accounted for in a manner similar to that for other exchanges, i.e., the assets acquired should be accounted for on the basis of the fair value of the consideration given or the fair value of the assets acquired.

Those who favor "pooling" accounting for a combination effected through an exchange of capital stock are convinced that no exchange transaction, in the normal sense of that term, has taken place, and that the accounting for the combination need not follow the pattern used to account for exchange transactions. Particular emphasis is placed (1) on the fact that, from the point of view of the two entities combined, there is no change of any substance in the assets, and (2) on the fact that the ownership interests of the two or more companies existing prior to the combination continue as ownership interests in the surviving entity. The conclusion, then, is that the accounting for the transaction should follow as closely as possible the existing bases of accountability which the formerly separate entities had maintained. The combination should not be accounted for in a manner similar to an exchange, since no exchange of any substance took place.

The issue here appears to be clearly drawn from a conceptual standpoint. Has an exchange transaction taken place significant enough to warrant an accounting treatment consistent with that accorded other exchange transactions, or is the transaction primarily one of form with so little substance that existing accountabilities should not be disturbed? While the results that flow from the conclusion reached on this issue will be divergent, the conclusion must be reached by analysis of the situation as it exists, without regard to the consequences. If the consequences flowing from the conclusion are inappropriate, inequitable, or inapplicable, accountants may not accept it on *practical* grounds, but must then recognize that their decision is unwarranted on *conceptual* grounds. To argue that a decision is conceptually sound, when in fact it is not, can only produce confusion and illogic in a framework which might otherwise be completely satisfactory.

At this point it seems appropriate to note once again that accounting reflects economic activity *in terms of the entity which produces the activity*. Accounting actions are not commonly made in terms of a group of ownership interests, but more commonly in terms of groups of economic assets or properties which a given ownership group may control. When an entity gains control over economic assets not formerly controlled by it, an accounting action is required. When the constituents of the ownership group change periodically, as they commonly do, and when this change results in little or no effect on the assets and properties in use, little or no accounting action is necessary to give effect to the change. When, however, the constituents of the ownership group change and the economic assets which the entity controls also change in a single transaction, some accounting action is necessary to give effect to the new assets which the entity controls.

In a business combination effected through an exchange of stock, two things happen: (1) the assets and liabilities of the entity are expanded, and (2) the ownership interests in the entity are expanded. If the transaction has resulted from arm's-length bargaining between independent parties, the entities involved should give effect to the transaction in a manner consistent with the treatment accorded other transactions in which the economic assets of an entity change. If, however, the transaction is lacking in substance, as when two formerly related companies combine their interests in what amounts merely to a change in legal form, no significant accounting action is required or desirable. Thus, the combinations which were forerunners of the present-day pooling accounting (see pages 22-23) were properly accounted for by use of pooling-of-interests accounting. The transference of this accounting action to combinations resulting from arm's-length dealing, however, was unwarranted from a conceptual viewpoint and resulted in accounting for a specific type of exchange transaction in a manner inconsistent with the accounting for other exchange transactions in which an entity engages.

It is our judgment that the weight of logic and consistency supports the conclusion that business combinations between independent entities are exchange transactions involving a transfer of assets and that the accounting action to account for an exchange transaction is necessary to reflect properly the results of the business transaction.

The Criteria

As we have noted, various criteria have been used in recent years to distinguish a pooling of interests from a purchase. Our study indicated that these criteria were artificial guidelines and in many instances did not provide substantive clues to the nature of the transaction. Our study also indicated a gradual deterioration in the criteria, so that the standards fluctuated from year to year. This was particularly true with the size criterion, which was at one time "approximately the same size," later became "90%-10% or 95%-5%" in *Accounting Research Bulletin No. 48*, and actually went to a comparative size relationship of 300 to 1 or more in practice.

We found that the vast majority of business combinations consummated in recent years involved constituents of disproportionate size. At the same time the pooling concept has become predominant in accounting for business combinations consummated by transfer of capital stock. Attempts to establish a relative-size criterion to distinguish "purchase" from "pooling" accounting have proved fruitless. In fact, virtually everyone with whom we discussed this matter agreed that no effective size criterion could be developed with any logical foundation.

The discussion in the next few sections will attempt to develop the

CHAPTER 7: ACCOUNTING FOR BUSINESS COMBINATIONS—TOWARD A SOLUTION

accounting action necessary to reflect properly the effect of a business combination. The discussion will develop the appropriate accounting action if the combination is considered to be a purchase and if it is considered to be a pooling of interests. The following chapter will consider more fully the consequences which would flow from the application of the alternative accounting actions and also consider several problems that would arise under the use of each alternative.

The following discussion is essentially based on the fact that the combination transaction involves a *dominant* entity in effect acquiring or combining with a *smaller* entity, regardless of the manner in which the combination is effected. The latter portion of the chapter introduces a concept of accounting for combinations which we call "fair-value pooling." This concept may be applicable in a few situations in which it is not clear as to which entity acquires the other and in which the resultant entity is materially different in size, scope of operations, and earning potential from any of its constituents.

Accounting for Assets Received

Purchase accounting. A wide range of exchange transactions is regularly accounted for through the application of the following formula: assets or equities acquired in an exchange transaction are recorded in terms of the money or the fair value of the other consideration given, or the fair value of the properties acquired, whichever is more clearly evident.[1]

In any exchange transaction, including a business combination, a variety of alternative bases may be available for recording the assets acquired.

1. Cash or cash equivalent of assets given up in exchange
2. Cash or cash equivalent of equities given up in exchange
3. Cash or cash equivalent of assets received in exchange
4. Book value of assets received in exchange, as that value exists in the accounting records of the transferor
5. Book value of assets or equities given in exchange

---

[1] American Institute of Certified Public Accountants, Committee on Accounting Procedure, *Accounting Research Bulletin No. 43*, Chapter 7c, "Business Combinations," p. 56. 1953. *Accounting Research Bulletin No. 48*, "Business Combinations," p. 24. 1957.

6. Par or stated value of the equities given up in exchange

The essence of the problem of choice among these alternatives seems to lie in the determination of the basis of accountability for those assets newly entering the control of the entity. The most logical basis appears to be the exchange price paid by the entity gaining control of the assets. Values existing by mere chance, such as the par or other stated value of equities given, or the values existing on a different entity's records at the exchange date, appear to have little, if any, relevance to the entity which newly assumes accountability for the assets.

A fair measure of the accountability for the service potential being acquired would appear to lie in the determination of the value of the service potential (assets or equities) being transferred in the exchange. Such a measure has relevance to the entity. If at times a measure of the value of the assets or equities given up in the exchange is not fairly determinable, a suitable alternative would appear to lie in the valuation of the service potential contained in the assets or resources received in exchange.

While the above conclusion may appear to be a mere restatement of the current generally accepted basis of accounting for exchange transactions, the fact remains that a fair consideration of the other alternatives listed leads to the conclusion that their relevance, and thus logic, is comparatively inappropriate. We should emphasize that the stated concept of accounting for exchange transactions is more broadly based than the commonly stated "cost" concept for exchange transactions. The above concept encompasses such measures as market price, fair value, and estimated value for those exchange transactions in which assets other than cash are being given up in the exchange.[2]

If the "exchange-price" concept developed above possesses the validity which it appears to have, the conclusion is evident that the manner in which an exchange transaction is consummated should have no effect upon the concept applicable to the transaction. The problem for *all* exchange transactions appears to lie in the determination of the fair value of the new assets or resources acquired.

When this general concept is applied to the problem of business combinations, the appropriate accounting action becomes evident. The

---

[2] Maurice Moonitz, "The Basic Postulates of Accounting," *Accounting Research Study No. 1,* pp. 28-31. American Institute of Certified Public Accountants. 1961.

assets or properties received in exchange for either cash, other assets, debt, or stock should be accounted for on the basis of the cash equivalent, or fair value, of the consideration given — the exchange price or purchase price.

Pooling accounting. When a business combination is deemed to be a pooling of interests, there is, in effect, a denial of an exchange transaction. Therefore, the reasoning used and conclusions developed above may not be appropriate. The transaction is viewed more as a pooling, merging, or combining of properties which were formerly accountable under separate entities into one entity. Whereas guides to accounting for exchange transactions are fairly widely recognized and accepted, guides to accounting for "pooling" transactions are not so widely recognized and understood. This is true, of course, because of the relatively small number of situations (other than business combinations) arising in business in which a "pooling" concept may be applicable.

Some accounting recognition must be accorded the assets received in the combination transaction. If the exchange basis developed above is considered to be inappropriate, it would appear that accounting for the assets received on the same basis that they were carried by the predecessor entity would be most appropriate. This conclusion follows logically from the manner in which the nature of the transaction is viewed. Since the view is that nothing of real economic substance has occurred in the transaction, an accounting treatment which continues the asset bases as they existed at the date of the transaction appears proper. This conclusion would not, however, prevent the correction of any asset bases which were known at the time to be inappropriate or which would result in inconsistencies in the accounting records subsequent to the combination. Thus, for example, correction of prior years' depreciation because of past use of inappropriate estimates of service lives would be desirable. Likewise, recognition of accounts receivable, net of estimated uncollectible accounts, would be appropriate even if the predecessor entity had formerly used a direct write-off method.

This method of accounting has been used and accepted for business combinations involving companies which are jointly owned. Since this type of situation does not appear to involve any changes of substance from the pre-existing circumstances, the accounting action described appears to be appropriate. Business combinations between formerly separate entities, when these combinations are viewed as involving no change of substance from the pre-existing circumstances, would therefore appear to require similar accounting recognition. We should also emphasize that the method of accounting described would not appear appropriate in combinations when, in fact, the transaction involved substantive changes from the pre-existing conditions. Thus, any combination involving a conveyance of assets, rather than stock, to effect the combination would not appear to meet the requirements for pooling accounting.

Summary. Substantially all business combinations, regardless of the manner in which they are consummated, result in exchange transactions. Therefore, we conclude that purchase accounting, as described above, provides the best clues to accounting for the assets received in exchange.

The existence of two generally accepted alternatives to account for assets acquired in a combination effected through the use of equities is illogical. Where equities are used to effect the exchange transaction, the general concept of valuing that which is received in the exchange at the fair value of the equities given up appears to be valid. Whether viewed from the point of view of the management or of the entity, proper accountability for the new properties appears to be best measured by the cash equivalent value of the equities transferred — the exchange price.

The above concept of asset accountability for combination transactions finds additional support in the fact that the combination is a significant event requiring proper accounting action. The assets acquired are in reality committed to a "fresh start" as far as their future use and management is concerned. Any acquisition of assets by an entity, whether new or used, represents a significant event for the entity. Proper accounting for this event requires an accounting treatment which recognizes a fair measure of the accountability for the assets acquired by the entity. Such a measure should properly reflect the "cost" of these assets to the entity. The existing book value of these assets has less significance to the entity than does a measure of the fair value of the outlay necessary to acquire the assets. The assets have, in effect, been granted a "fresh start," and their fair value to the acquiring entity as of the date of the fresh start is of primary significance.

Accounting for Consideration Given

Purchase accounting. If assets are used as consideration in the transaction, no new problem arises because they would be removed from

CHAPTER 7: ACCOUNTING FOR BUSINESS COMBINATIONS—TOWARD A SOLUTION

the records and the resultant gain or loss recorded. When capital stock is used to effect the exchange, however, a problem is encountered because the American Institute of Certified Public Accountants has long had a rule which states:

> 3. Earned surplus of a subsidiary company created prior to acquisition does not form a part of the consolidated earned surplus of the parent company and subsidiaries; nor can any dividend declared out of such surplus properly be credited to the income account of the parent company.[3]

This rule dates back to 1933 and arose in the aftermath of the financial excesses of the late 1920's. For nearly twenty years this rule was widely accepted. To many the basic soundness of the rule appeared evident, and little criticism was heard. The rule appears to be a logical adjunct to the concept of accounting for exchange transactions effected through the transfer of stock. The retained earnings (earned surplus) reported by a given entity should represent past earnings of that entity not yet distributed in the form of dividends or capitalized in some legal manner. Since the assets newly acquired have not yet had an opportunity to generate earnings for the entity, it would appear to be unsound to increase the retained earnings account at the time the new assets enter the entity's accountability.

The basic reason behind the above rule appears to flow from the concept of an entity. The accounting entity is generally conceived of as a group of resources committed to a variety of purposes. The entity comes into existence with the initial dedication of a group of resources to a specific economic endeavor or endeavors. The resources of this entity are in a constant state of change as those who manage the resources utilize them in various business activities. One means by which the resources of the entity change is by expanding operations through the acquisition of new resources. One type of acquisition may involve a combination with another entity.

These new resources, as yet unused by the acquiring entity, cannot possibly have generated any earned surplus for that entity. Any earned surplus existing on the books of the acquired entity has no relevance to the entity now owning the resources or to its management. To add this earned surplus to that existing on the records of a different accounting entity would render the resultant earned surplus nonhomogeneous.

---

[3] American Institute of Certified Public Accountants, Committee on Accounting Procedure, *Accounting Research Bulletin No. 43*, Chapter 1a, "Rules Adopted by Membership," p. 11. 1953.

Thus, the proper accounting for the consideration given in a business combination transaction determined to be an exchange would be: (1) increase Capital Stock for the par or stated value of the stock transferred in the exchange, and (2) record any excess (or deficiency) in a paid-in or capital surplus account, generally more specifically labeled "Excess of issue price over par or stated value of stock issued." The sum of (1) and (2) would, of course, be equal to the fair value of the consideration given in the combination transaction.

Pooling accounting. One of the features of pooling-of-interests accounting is the possibility of carrying forward of the combined retained earnings of the constituents as retained earnings of the resultant entity. In the late 1940's and early 1950's there was some feeling that this procedure was a contradiction of the AICPA rule cited above (page 78). However, *Accounting Research Bulletin No. 48* recognized this deviation from the general rule, but asserted that, in effect, no deviation actually existed, because under the pooling concept the new enterprise was regarded as a continuation of all the constituent corporations. No acquisition had been made; the continuation of one legal entity in a subsidiary relationship to another was a mere convenience without real substance.

Thus, *Accounting Research Bulletin No. 48* approved the carrying forward of the retained earnings of the constituents in a pooling combination. This conclusion appears to be a logical outgrowth of the concept of a pooling which we developed earlier. If the combination is deemed to be a mere continuation in one entity of two formerly separate entities, the retained earnings of the resultant entity should be the sum of the retained earnings of the constituents, unless capitalized. The objections frequently interposed against this procedure generally are based upon the context of the previously cited AICPA rule or upon an inconsistency with the entity concept. Our prior discussion has emphasized, however, that those who favor pooling accounting would look upon the resultant entity as a continuation of the constituent entities, i.e., would view them as if they had always been a part of one "entity family."

Thus, the proper accounting for the consideration given in a business combination transaction determined to be a pooling would be to increase

1. Capital Stock for par or stated value of the stock given.
2. Paid-in or Capital Surplus for an amount equal to the capital surplus of the acquired company, plus or minus any adjustment neces-

sitated by differences in par or stated value of the capital stock accounts.

3. Retained Earnings for the retained earnings of the acquired company, less any adjustments necessary (1) to absorb an excess of the par or stated value of capital stock given over the par or stated value of capital stock received plus applicable paid-in or capital surplus, or (2) to absorb any asset adjustments deemed necessary at the time of the combination transaction.

Summary. Earned surplus of an entity should represent past earnings of the entity not yet distributed through board action. In a business combination deemed to be an exchange transaction and regardless of whether the acquired entity remains in existence as a subsidiary, the fact is that one entity has acquired another. The resultant entity now has additional assets, additional service resources, for which it is accountable. Since these assets were acquired in an exchange transaction, and since earned surplus properly arises only from profitable use of the operating (service) resources, an increase in the earned surplus of the resultant entity at the time of the business combination transaction is not logical.

If the combination is viewed as a pooling of interests, strong practical arguments can be made, however, for reporting the earned surplus on a combined basis. If this practice is to be followed, accountants must recognize that its use injects a practical deviation from a soundly based accounting concept into the accounting process.

At this point it is well to note that several states have laws which appear to act to prevent the combining of retained earnings accounts. In some states dividends are restricted to amounts earned by the given corporation as a separate legal entity. In other states earned surplus of one company may be combined with that of another if the combination is effected in a certain manner. Other states have still different provisions in this area. Nevertheless, accountants can still employ a concept of "earned surplus" which ignores these variations in local law and can disclose "surplus available for dividends" if it differs from the earned surplus. While it may be desirable that accounting concepts and legal precepts be in agreement, it does not necessarily follow that otherwise sound accounting actions should be rejected in favor of legal concepts not soundly grounded from an accounting viewpoint. "Surplus available for dividends" in accordance with applicable legal provisions can be clearly disclosed in financial statements.

The Fair Value Pooling Concept

If one accepts the proposition that business combination transactions are basically exchange transactions, a problem arises in certain combinations wherein the facts are not clear as to which constituent acquires the other. These situations would normally arise when the constituents are relatively the same size.

The discussion of purchase accounting earlier in this chapter was built upon the framework of the accounting entity and the critical nature of the business transaction as related to the entity. A substantial majority of the business combinations that are consummated involve constituents of disproportionate size. The conclusions reached were based upon the fact that the combination transaction involves an "exchange" in which the dominant entity in effect acquires a smaller business entity.

The conclusion that business combinations should, in effect, be accounted for in the same manner as any exchange transaction has substantial logical support. This appears true even though the application of this accounting treatment produces asset values in the resultant entity on two different bases: original cost, less amortization, for those assets which the acquiring company had in use at the date of combination, and current or fair value for those assets newly acquired in the combination. This phenomenon would be true regardless of whether the form of the transaction had A acquire B, or had C, a new legal entity, acquire both A and B if, in fact, A did acquire B. Many accountants with whom we held discussions indicated that the merging of the assets at different values was unsound and that the "purchase" treatment created an inconsistency in balance sheet values. Their conclusion was that "pooling" accounting should be used in order to state the various assets on similar bases.

It is not the purchase method of accounting for combinations, however, which produces the diversity of asset values. Asset values are constantly changing as prices change, as combinations of assets in use prove more or less valuable than operation of the assets separately, as well as from a variety of other causes. Accountants normally do not give effect to changing asset values, regardless of the cause, unless the entity engages in some event which provides an objective basis upon which to record the change. Thus, unrealized appreciation in assets arising when prices increase is normally given no accounting recognition. Many times it is this fact of price fluctuations which causes identical assets to have different accounting bases, if they enter an entity's accountability at different times.

Accountants who object to the varying asset bases resulting from purchase accounting for combinations should recognize that an alternative other than the existing "pooling-of-interests" accounting is possible. The *acquiring* company's assets might be stated on a current value basis to coincide with the basis of the newly acquired assets rather than recording the new assets on a basis that existed on a different entity's records. This accounting procedure might be referred to as "fair value" pooling and may be useful in some combinations.

A small minority of the business combinations we studied involved constituents of relatively the same size. In such a combination the facts may be so unclear as to make it difficult to contend that one entity acquired another. Therefore, even though the basic nature of the combination remains an exchange transaction, it may be inappropriate to account for it as if one entity acquired control over the assets and properties of another. Combinations of constituents which are relatively the same size create a resultant entity which is generally materially different in nature, scope of operations, control over resources and personnel, and even in methods of operation from either of the previous business units. In effect the resultant entity is a new business — one materially different from either pre-existing business.

In combinations which result in an essentially new enterprise there may be nothing inherent in prior carrying values to warrant their continued usage subsequent to the combination. Rather, it is possible that the assets of the resultant entity should be accounted for based on their "cost" to the new entity. Since the accounting unit is, in effect, a new entity, cost to the entity would involve a determination of the fair value of the assets contributed to the future use of the entity. All the assets would be carried forward at their fair value at the date the new entity came into being (the date of the combination). Likewise, the resultant entity would report no earned surplus until such time as its operations generated earnings.

The "fair value" pooling concept is not presented as an alternative to the concepts of accounting for business combinations developed earlier in this chapter. Rather, it is a concept which may be most descriptive of the situation resulting from a few business combinations wherein the resultant enterprise is, in essence, a new enterprise. The accounting aspects of this concept — restatement of the assets in terms of current fair values and elimination of earned surplus — might also, however, be applicable in situations other than the relatively few business combinations for which they might be appropriate. For example, the occurrence of any event which might indicate an entity had made, in essence, a fresh start could result in such restatement of asset values and elimination of earned surplus (deficit). Likewise, situations sometimes arise in which the book values of assets fail to reflect on a realistic basis the fair value of the unused service potential which the assets possess. Asset restatement on a fair value basis to achieve, in effect, a fresh start might be appropriate here.

The applicability of the "fair value" pooling concept may be illustrated by considering two practical situations. Does a combination involving two grocery stores, for example, of relatively the same size produce "a significantly different" resultant entity, or is it necessary that the constituents be involved in different types of operations? It seems to us that a combination of any two entities of relatively the same size will produce a new business entity. The fact that the constituents were in the same line of business prior to the combination would not prevent the combination from producing a "new" entity. The "new" entity can be "new" in the sense of a significant change in nature, a significant change in scope, or a significant change in asset control or earning power.

Does a combination involving several constituents, no one of which is relatively the same size as the largest constituent but the sum total of which is to produce a "significantly different" business entity, warrant "fair value" pooling treatment? What if the series of combinations is a part of an over-all expansion plan of one constituent? Both of these questions pose difficult problems. However, if the total effect of the combination transactions produces a resultant entity significantly different from any of the constituents, the "fair value" pooling treatment would be indicated. A review of all the attendant circumstances would be necessary prior to the determination of a final decision. The judgment must be based upon consummated actions, not on anticipations of future events. We must recognize that business combinations, no matter how insignificant, do not take place in a vacuum or in the absence of negotiation and serious consideration by the participants. A review of these negotiations, of all the circumstances surrounding the actions taken and contemplated, should provide the professional accountant with the basis for rendering a sound judgment regarding the transaction.

One modification of the "fair value" pooling concept would be to carry forward earned surplus in the financial statements of the resultant entity. While this modification does not appear to follow logically from the reasoning developed earlier, it may have practical application in some circumstances.

CHAPTER 7: ACCOUNTING FOR BUSINESS COMBINATIONS—TOWARD A SOLUTION

The following comparison may be made between the existing concept of accounting for a "pooling of interests," the "fair value" pooling concept presented above, and the modification of this latter concept.

1. The concept of "pooling" used in the past would account for assets on the basis of their existing book values on the records of the constituents at the date of combination. Likewise, the combined earned surplus balances of the constituents could be carried forward as earned surplus of the resultant entity. This treatment would be applicable whether the combination resulted in the emergence of one legal entity subsequent to the combination or the continuance of each constituent as a legal entity, one in a subsidiary position to the other.

2. The concept of "fair value" pooling developed above would account for the assets of the resultant enterprise at their fair value as of the date of the combination. The fair value would be determined by consideration of all available data at that date, with primary emphasis attaching to the negotiations coincident to the exchange transaction, appraised values, and other pertinent information bearing upon a determination of fair value. Under this concept the resultant enterprise would carry forward no earned surplus, since the enterprise is a new business entity, regardless of the legal status of the resultant entity. This treatment of earned surplus would be similar to that arising under the quasi-reorganization procedure for "downward" reorganizations. Earned surplus legally available for dividends would be reported in an appropriate manner.

3. A third concept, a combination of the first two, would account for the assets of the resultant enterprise at their fair value as of the date of combination, this basis determinable as outlined above. The resultant entity would carry forward as earned surplus the combined earned surpluses of the constituents, except for necessary adjustments occasioned by the combination.

For those relatively few combinations in which the economic result is, in effect, a new enterprise, the weight of logic and of consistency with other accounting concepts supports the second of these alternatives. The principal justification, conceptually, would be that the combination produces an entirely new business entity. As such, the values existing in the accounting records of the various constituents at the date of combination would appear to have little relevance to the new entity. The accounting problem involved would be similar to

CHAPTER 7: THE FAIR VALUE POOLING CONCEPT

• that arising in the formation of a new business through contribution of various properties by various ownership interests. In such a situation neither existing book values nor par nor other stated values of equity interests issued have particular relevance in assigning accountability to the properties contributed. Fair value of the assets contributed does have prime relevance in such a situation. In fact, the problem of asset valuation in a combination resulting in a "totally new situation" would not be as difficult as that in formation of a new enterprise through various asset contributions. The negotiations coincident to the combination would provide far better clues to the appropriate asset valuation than might exist in the latter situation.

Relating this concept to that accepted in the quasi-reorganization procedure also appears relevant. It is true that the quasi-reorganization procedure has been applied generally only to entities in financial difficulties with the objective generally being to eliminate an accumulated deficit and to adjust asset values to a more realistic basis. The entity is given a "fresh start," placing it on a basis much as if it were a new entity.

There does not appear to be any logical reason, however, to limit the quasi-reorganization procedure to the above situation. If the attendant circumstances appear to warrant a "fresh start" or appear to support a conclusion that an existing entity has so changed its nature, scope of operations, or earning potential as to be, in effect, a new entity, the quasi-reorganization procedure may be applicable. Certainly a business combination wherein the constituents were approximately the same in size and scope of operations, so that neither in reality "acquired" the other, could well produce a business entity significantly different from any of the constituents in the combination.

A logical extension of this concept would indicate that the resultant entity should carry forward no earned surplus following the combination. We recognize, however, that the analogy to a quasi-reorganization is not complete. Furthermore, in many situations valid reasons may exist for carrying forward the amount of earned surplus legally available for dividends. Thus, the third alternative may well be appropriate to reflect properly certain combinations. In any event, if the earned surplus carried forward differs materially from the amount of surplus available for dividends, this latter amount may be disclosed parenthetically. Subsequent earnings of the resultant enterprise would not necessitate separate disclosure.

• For those combinations which result in a new enterprise the first alternative listed above (the pooling of interests) has little support from either a conceptual or logical viewpoint. This alternative has the practical effect of carrying forward asset values not properly reflective of the fair value of the assets committed to use by the entity. Financial reports resulting from the application of this alternative in the combination situation described would tend to be misleading and **not** representative of the substance of the transaction.

8

Accounting for Business Combinations— Consequences of Alternatives

Varying consequences arise from the application of either of the two major alternative methods of accounting for business combinations presented in the preceding chapter. This chapter considers these consequences as well as some of the problems created by the application of the alternative concepts. The consequences of the application of the "fair value" pooling concept will be given only limited discussion since this concept would be applicable to a small number of combinations and since most of the consequences which would flow from application of this concept will be considered in discussing purchase accounting and pooling accounting.

Consequences of Purchase Accounting

Goodwill. Probably the consequence of purchase accounting which is subject to the greatest criticism is the emergence in the accounting of an item frequently labeled "goodwill." Throughout our discussions with various accountants we consistently heard that purchase accounting was undesirable because it created goodwill. While we have commented on this issue at some length previously, a few additional comments are appropriate here.

As noted in chapter 6 (page 56), we found that in combinations studied which were accounted for as purchases, the excess of fair value over book value was allocated or assigned to specific tangibles and intangibles (other than goodwill) as frequently as it was described as goodwill. We would reiterate that in an exchange transaction as significant as most business combinations are the negotiation proceedings and bargaining bases will frequently provide sound clues for allocating the fair value determined among the various properties acquired. In traditional consolidating procedures accountants have become accustomed over the years to attaching the convenient goodwill label to the excess of cost (fair value) over the book value of the equity acquired. A more careful review of this excess may well provide the basis for a more accurate description of the amount. On the other hand, part or all of the excess will properly be described as goodwill in a number of combinations.

Unquestionably the most significant objection to the "creation" of goodwill lies in the existing policy on amortization of the amount that is recorded. (Amortization creates additional consequences which will be discussed at greater length below.) Amortization of any asset is supportable to the extent that (a) the asset contributes to earnings in a given period and in so doing loses a portion of its potential service contribution, or (b) the asset loses a portion of its service potential without making any particular contribution. The amortization of goodwill merely to get the amount eliminated from the balance sheet within a given period of time is not logically sound, even though it may result in a more conservative appearing balance sheet.

We recognize that past experiences (particularly in the late 20's and early 30's) with the recognition of goodwill and its subsequent write-off were unpleasant. However, the fact remains that the balance sheet of an entity should reflect all assets of the entity to the extent they possess service potential for the future. The conservative approach to the amortization of goodwill, which is evident in Chapter 5 of *Accounting Research Bulletin No. 43*, has undoubtedly influenced accountants to prevent the recognition of goodwill, if this is at all possible. A re-evaluation of this conservative policy on amortization of goodwill could well indicate that the emphasis on amortization has resulted in arbitrary or advance write-offs of goodwill to an extent which is not supportable.

Dilution of earnings per share. As implied above, the persistent objection to the recognition of goodwill likely has a basis other than an objection to goodwill *per se*. This objection lies in the effect of the

CHAPTER 8: CONSEQUENCES OF PURCHASE ACCOUNTING

amortization of goodwill on earnings. The following example will illustrate this situation:

	Co. A	Co. B
Net Assets	$5,000,000	$300,000
Capital Stock, Par $10 Per Share	$3,000,000	$200,000
Retained Earnings	2,000,000	100,000
	$5,000,000	$300,000
Book Value Per Share	$16.67	$15.00
Net Income for Past Year	$450,000	$30,000
Earnings Per Share	$1.50	$1.50

First, assume that the negotiations resulted in an agreement that Co. A would acquire all of the stock of Co. B on a basis of one share of Co. A's stock for each share of Co. B's stock. Each company was earning about the same rate, and an even exchange was agreeable. Assume further that the negotiations indicated that all assets of Co. B were fairly valued, and also that Co. A's stock was selling for about $15 per share in the market. Here all evidence would support Co. A recording the combination exchange at about $300,000, or an amount equal to the book value of Co. B's stock. Amortization of the assets acquired would presumably follow a pattern similar to that followed by Co. B. If business and competitive conditions remained the same, Co. A would likely be able to report per share earnings of about $1.50 in the year after combination. ($480,000 combined income ÷ 320,000 shares.)

Now assume that the negotiation proceedings resulted in an agreement that Co. A would acquire all the stock of Co. B on a basis of 1.5 shares of Co. A's stock for each share of Co. B's stock. A number of reasons might explain the relative undervaluation of A's stock: relative bargaining abilities, differences in market values of stock, undervaluation of B's assets, "assets" of unrecorded Co. B, such as valuable patents or other franchises, good management, location, etc. Whatever the reason, it seems most reasonable to assume that from the negotiation proceedings accountants should be able to determine the explanation of the apparent disparity.

Assume further that the market value per share of Co. A's stock was $15, with a fair value of Co. B's net assets of $450,000. Now Co. A would be accountable for assets of $450,000, and this amount would have to be allocated among the tangible and intangible assets of Co. B. Assuming that this amount was all allocable to assets subject to amortization, Co. A would charge against the next year's income an amount greater than Co. B had been charging. Thus, for example, if Co. B had been allocating the cost of its $300,000 net assets over ten years ($30,000 per year), Co. A would allocate $45,000 in the next year, provided the ten-year basis was deemed appropriate. Earnings per share of Co. A would then be $1.41 [($480,000 − $15,000) divided by 330,000 shares]. The decrease in earnings of $.09 per share would be a "dilution" of earnings. If we recognize the importance attached to the maintenance or increase of earnings per share, we can recognize the significance of this end result. The same result would be obtained if the excess of fair value of Co. B's net assets over their book value were determined to be goodwill and if this goodwill were amortized on a ten-year basis.

This is a consequence which has great practical importance, and from our research appears to have been an important consideration in the relative decline in application of the purchase concept to business combinations. One cannot criticize the desire of management to prevent such "dilutions" in earnings. However, it appears not only eminently fair and equitable, but also essential from an accounting point of view, to report dilutions of this type *if they do occur*. The use of accounting procedures and practices which *artificially* maintain earnings per share is both illogical and inequitable to all parties concerned.

We feel the following conclusions on this point are appropriate:

1. If the combination exchange results in a higher basis for the assets acquired than their former book value, and if this increased basis is attributable to assets subject to amortization, it is incumbent upon accountants to reflect these facts regardless of the effect on per share earnings.

2. If the combination exchange results in a higher basis for the assets acquired than their former book value, and if the increased basis is attributable to assets not subject to amortization (to assets whose service value is not impaired through operations), accountants should not arbitrarily amortize the excess and thereby create a dilution in earnings per share.

We would emphasize that accountants must be guided in this area by proper accounting for assets, regardless of the effect of this accounting on earnings per share. The effect on earnings per share of the decision on amortization of assets should in no way influence the decision.

Emphasis on market value per share. Many critics of purchase accounting emphasize that the purchase concept carries an implication that the fair value of the assets acquired will be based on the market value of the stock given in the exchange. They further emphasize that market values are subject to the vagaries of the market place, are constantly fluctuating, and are not necessarily appropriate bases to use in the valuation of the assets received in a combination exchange. We cannot disagree with these latter propositions. We must disagree, however, with the basic premise that the purchase concept involves an implication that market values of the stock transferred be used. Market value is only one of several possible bases, although it is unquestionably one of the most apparent and easiest to determine.

We see nothing sacred in the use of market value of the shares given to determine the fair value of the assets acquired. Rather, we insist that this value is determinable from a review of all aspects of the negotiation proceedings, and that market value of the shares given is only one of the considerations. The negotiations preceding eventual consummation of a business combination commonly involve considerable bargaining regarding the inherent value of the properties involved. Even though the hardest bargaining may be over the *relative* values of the properties being merged, each party makes a more or less thorough evaluation of what it is receiving and giving. The accountants participating in these negotiations should then have available considerable information to provide a reasonably sound basis for determining the fair value of the properties exchanged.

Admittedly, the degree of objectivity attaching to the real fair value in the combination may be less than that existing in the market value of the stock given (or the book value of the assets acquired). The difficulty of arriving at fair value, however, should not obscure the basic issue. While market value of the shares issued (or book value of the assets acquired) may be readily determinable, the fact is that neither may provide a sound basis for reflecting the exchange value of the assets acquired. Overstatement and understatement of asset values are equally objectionable. Determination of the fair value of assets acquired may not be as simple as determination of other accounting bases, but it is essential that accountants strive to make such a determination for transactions as significant as business combinations.

Nonhomogeneous asset valuations. Another commonly asserted undesirable consequence of purchase accounting is that it results in the reporting of "nonhomogeneous" asset values on the balance sheet. This assertion certainly cannot be refuted. The acquisition, however, of virtually all assets in times of changing prices and changing technology produces "nonhomogeneous" asset values. This consequence is not peculiar to accounting for business combinations and does not provide a sound basis for criticism of purchase accounting in this area. Even "pooling" accounting will produce a degree of nonhomogeneity in financial statements, since the acquired company normally would not have acquired its assets in the same periods as the acquiring company.

Whenever an entity engages in an exchange transaction the acquired property will be reported at the then current value. Likewise, existing properties which the entity owns are not restated to reflect then current values. The consequence is nonhomogeneous asset valuation. While the significance of this consequence may be greater as a result of a business combination transaction, the end result is not peculiar to such transactions.

Retained earnings. Accounting for business combinations as purchases results in carrying forward only the retained earnings of the acquiring entity. As noted earlier, however, some objections have been raised as to the equity of this result. We should note that the exchange price in the combination reflects the inherent asset values of the acquired company. To the extent that assets generated by past earnings have not yet been distributed as dividends the shares issued in the exchange will be greater than if earnings had been distributed. Thus, the acquired company's shareholders are in effect receiving a return of their past undistributed profits through the medium of the additional shares transferred in the exchange.

As for the acquiring entity, there appears to be no justification for augmenting its retained earnings because it entered into a transaction to acquire additional properties. The combination transaction can in no way affect past earnings not yet distributed. Any significant variance between retained earnings from an accounting viewpoint and earned surplus from a legal viewpoint can be disclosed adequately in the notes to financial statements.

Consequences of Pooling Accounting

Goodwill write-off. The application of pooling accounting to business combinations results in recording asset values for properties acquired at the same values as those existing on the acquired company's books. If the fair value of the exchange transaction indicates that the acquiring company in effect paid for goodwill, no recognition of this value is reflected in the accounting entry. The effect is to omit accountability for goodwill. Pooling accounting, therefore, produces the same end effect as would recognition of the goodwill followed by a direct write-off to some surplus account.

Since the issuance of *Accounting Research Bulletin No. 43* in 1953, the direct write-off of goodwill to capital surplus has been unacceptable. This policy is consistent with the concept that capital surplus (or earned surplus, for that matter) should not absorb charges which would otherwise be made against income. The pooling concept produces the same result which the committee on accounting procedure found objectionable in 1953.

> Thus by a piece of conservative balance sheet accounting, in in which the newly acquired assets are carried at a comparatively low value, the income statement is relieved of charges to amortize the goodwill that would have been recorded as an asset if the transaction had been accounted for as a purchase.
>
> ... the effect is to nullify the accounting principles requiring substantially all charges to go through the income account. Here the charge to eliminate the goodwill is, in effect, made in advance. It is made not to income and not to earned surplus, but to capital surplus or the capital account, through the convenient device of never recording the goodwill by never recording the full consideration for which the capital stock was issued.[1]

Asset misstatement. The vast majority of business combination transactions reviewed in this research study possessed characteristics strongly indicative of an exchange transaction. The use of pooling accounting under these circumstances produces a convenient basis for asset recognition, but one which cannot be supported logically. The result is to state the newly acquired assets on a basis relevant to the acquired entity, but not necessarily relevant to the entity acquiring control.

The result of this procedure for an exchange transaction is a misstatement of the proper asset values. During the past ten years this misstatement has commonly been an understatement, although the reverse situation could arise when the fair value of assets acquired was less than the existing book values. While the conclusion as to

---

[1] Homer Kripke, "A Good Look at Goodwill in Corporate Acquisitions," *Banking Law Journal,* Dec. 1961, p. 1034.

whether pooling accounting results in a misstatement of asset values is arguable, the conclusion that misstatement of asset values is improper is not. We have noted earlier that the concept of a business combination as an exchange transaction would lead to a conclusion that application of pooling accounting usually results in asset misstatement. On the other hand, denial of the combination as an exchange transaction would lead to the conclusion that pooling accounting usually results in appropriate asset bases.

Possibly the most serious consequence of pooling accounting in this regard is the fact that its application on a regular basis conditions accountants against a thorough review of the inherent value of the tangible and specific intangible assets of the acquired company. *Accounting Research Bulletin No. 48* states clearly that the application of pooling accounting should not prevent adjustment of asset values which are misstated or adjustments necessary to conform the accounting records of the constituents. The ease and simplicity of the pooling method, however, could well result in statement of the asset values at their former book value without the careful review of the negotiation proceedings which is necessary to proper determination of the fair asset values.

Earnings per share. The importance attached to the maintenance of earnings per share appears to have been one significant consideration lending support to pooling accounting. In fact, we were told time and again in our field work that if earnings per share subsequent to the combination could not be maintained at a level at least equal to the earnings per share prior to the combination, the deal would not take place. For the management of the acquiring company this aspect of the combination is particularly important.

As pooling accounting achieved wider applicability in the 1950's and its consequences became better understood, increasing pressures developed for its application to an even wider range of combination transactions. To businessmen convinced that combinations *per se* are advantageous, the accountant who insisted on the application of purchase accounting proved to be a stumbling block. The question we heard frequently was: Why should accountants be able to prevent the occurrence of a desirable business transaction by their insistence on an inflexible accounting procedure?

In the absence of well-defined or logical criteria to use for guidance in the area and recognizing the atmosphere of the business community, one can readily understand the increasing acceptance of pooling accounting. As long as business conditions do not become adverse and if the new management (many times the same management) can maintain the existing efficiency of operations, earnings per share would not be impaired by the combination transaction. Recognition of higher asset values subject to amortization would, of course, have the effect of diminishing previous earnings per share.

The unusual significance attached to earnings per share and the ramifications it has in the financial world are undisputed conditions which accountants must recognize. Accountants likewise must, and do, recognize the widespread use of financial statements by various segments of our society. Those users have the right to conclude that the results portrayed in the financial statements are fair representations of the entity's financial position and results of operations. If the combination transaction is viewed as an exchange, pooling accounting will generally tend to result in a somewhat artificial maintenance of earnings per share, a result which accountants should not sanction. On the other hand, if the combination transaction is viewed principally as a change of economic form with little or no change of substance, pooling accounting will tend to result in an earnings per share presentation which reasonably portrays the results of the combined operations.

Once again, it appears evident that accountants must come to a proper conclusion on the basic nature of the transaction. The appropriate accounting action will flow from this conclusion. That the action taken results in maintenance, diminution, or increase of earnings per share should have no significant bearing on the accounting action to be taken to produce the end result.

Bargaining position. The determination of relative bargaining position of the constituents in any exchange transaction is difficult to assess or to define in general terms. However, our research did indicate a few generalizations which appear reasonable. For example, the stockholders of the selling company will generally accept shares of stock having a total market value lower than the amount of cash they would alternatively accept. This fact, of course, may be attributable to the income tax regulations under which no tax is currently due if the exchange involves shares of stock (with certain limitations), whereas a tax on any gain would be due immediately if cash were the basic medium used in the exchange. The fact that a growth in value of the shares received is anticipated also might contribute to this phenomenon.

The bargaining position of the management of the acquiring company may likewise be affected by the manner of effecting the transaction. The management may be willing to give up more value in terms of shares of stock than they would give up in cash. In fact, a great many combinations that have been consummated would likely never have taken place if the only medium of exchange were cash.

The acceptance of pooling accounting may also contribute to the share value to be given up once shares are determined to be the medium of exchange to be used. Since the amount for which management is accountable (i.e., the asset values to be recorded and subsequently amortized) is relatively unaffected by the number of shares to be given in a pooling combination, one possible pressure on the acquiring company management to drive a hard bargain is lacking. We have previously noted that the effect of the exchange on earnings per share in subsequent periods is a prime consideration of the acquiring company management. This factor tends to set an upper limit of the number of shares the acquiring company will issue.

We noted above that pooling accounting tends to maintain earnings per share at their precombination level. Purchase accounting, on the other hand, will tend, in times of rising prices, to reduce earnings per share below their previous levels. This reduction in earnings per share could be offset, in part at least, by issuance of fewer shares than might otherwise be used. Thus, it is submitted that the management of the acquiring company might feel impelled to drive a harder bargain as to the basis for the share transfer if it knew that purchase accounting were to be applied to the transaction. While there is no empirical evidence on this point, the conclusion appears reasonable based upon the frequent contention that if purchase accounting had been required uniformly in the past, numerous combinations would never have been consummated. The fact that pooling accounting could be used during the 1950's prevents any determination of the actual effect on management's bargaining position which a requirement for purchase accounting might have had.

Problems Arising from Adoption of Purchase Accounting

Determination of fair value. Certainly one of the more serious accounting problems to be faced under application of purchase accounting to business combinations is the determination of fair value. While this problem has been raised earlier in this report, we should emphasize here that the major consideration in solving this problem lies in a thorough review of the negotiation discussions. We found most accountants equating fair value with market value of the shares issued in the exchange. This measure of fair value may be appropriate in many circumstances. In others, however, the market value may be unduly inflated or depressed or may be unrepresentative of the fair value of the assets involved. For example, a market quotation of $50 for a share of X Co. stock may not be appropriate to use if 20,000 shares are given in exchange, since a block of this many shares might be transferable only at reduced prices.

The negotiation discussions, while possibly not producing as readily determinable a basis, should provide sufficient data upon which fair value of the assets received may be determined. Accountants face similar problems in accounting for donated assets and assets received from stockholders in exchange for a given number of shares of stock. Practical difficulties need not necessarily obscure the inherent merit in a given approach to solving a specific problem.

Bargain purchases. Several people raised with us the question of proper accounting for bargain purchases. Purchases of this type arise when, for a variety of reasons, the acquiring company is able to acquire another company at a price or upon terms which appear to be unusually favorable — bargains, in effect. The problem appears to arise from the fact that many accountants have felt that application of purchase accounting presumes the use of market value of shares issued as the proper basis of accountability. We have emphasized above, however, that this presumption does not always have validity. The principle in "bargain" situations should be the same as in other business combinations. The basis of accountability should reflect as closely as possible the fair value of the assets acquired. In bargain purchases, therefore, the assets acquired should be accounted for on the basis of the best approximation of fair value that is available from the negotiation proceedings.

The reasoning presented here is comparable to that which would apply for assets received as a donation or received as a partial donation with a nominal cash outlay. In purchase combinations in which cash is the medium for effecting the transaction there is, of course, a strong presumption that the cash outlay reflects the fair value of that which is acquired. When the facts of the combination indicate that this presumption lacks validity, proper accounting would reflect the assets received at the best approximation of fair value at that date which is available.

CHAPTER 8: ACCOUNTING FOR BUSINESS COMBINATIONS—CONSEQUENCES OF ALTERNATIVES

Amortization of goodwill. To summarize our conclusions on the proper treatment of the excess of fair value of consideration given over book value of assets acquired, (1) any portion of the excess which is attributable to tangible assets or specific intangibles other than goodwill should be amortized over the appropriate period of useful life, (2) any portion attributable to goodwill which appears to have limited value should be amortized over the period of expected limited life, and (3) any portion attributable to goodwill which does not appear to have limited life should be carried forward to future periods until evidence exists that the value is impaired. We must emphasize that careful consideration of the transaction is necessary at the time of its consummation to determine (1) the fair value of the assets acquired, and (2) the allocation of the fair value among appropriate assets. We would discourage adoption of convenient practices the results of which would fail to reflect as accurately as possible the essence of the transaction as consummated.

Problems Arising from Adoption of Pooling Accounting

Most of the problems which presently exist in pooling accounting center around the determination of the combinations which qualify for pooling accounting treatment. Our conclusions on this aspect of the problem have been set forth previously.

Prevailing practice in the combination area, however, is to consider substantially all combinations effected solely by the issuance of equity shares as poolings of interests. Exceptions to this practice are found in some combinations involving extremely wide divergence in the relative size of the constituents, in some combinations in which fair value and book value of assets involved are substantially the same, and in some combinations in which evidence clearly indicates that ownership and/or management continuity will be absent subsequent to the combination. The logical support for pooling accounting is commonly based on the contention that nothing of substance has happened in the situation, and therefore existing relationships should not be upset by an accounting entry. The discussion to follow will attempt to give fair consideration to several recurrent problems which arise under this concept of pooling of interests.

Part cash and part securities. Combinations involving partly cash and partly common stock are fairly common. Some evidence exists that in the early stage of the development of pooling accounting the existence of cash in the transaction was presumptive evidence that the combination was an exchange for which purchase accounting was appropriate. Gradually, this conclusion became modified until at present the existence of a relatively small portion of cash in the transaction will not necessarily prevent the use of pooling accounting. In all likelihood, this development was conditioned by provisions of the Internal Revenue Code dealing with tax-free reorganizations. Under these regulations cash up to 20% of the exchange price may be transferred without the transaction being disqualified as a tax-free exchange.

In combinations in which the acquiring company gave up both cash and common stock, we found three alternative accounting methods used: (1) purchase accounting for the entire transaction, (2) pooling accounting for the entire transaction, and (3) purchase accounting for the cash portion and pooling accounting for the stock portion. The reasoning for acceptance of the third alternative was based in large measure on the previous general acceptance of pooling accounting in a wide variety of situations. These situations involved a diversity of conditions under which pooling accounting had been applied. Thus, one could generally find a basis in past practice to support a situation only slightly different from an earlier pooling.

While many accountants may find a measure of logical support for pooling accounting in combinations involving an exchange of equity shares, it appears doubtful if similar logical support can be asserted for combinations in which cash is transferred. It is difficult to contend that nothing of substance has occurred in the transaction when the acquiring company has made a cash outlay. As the portion of cash transferred increases, this conclusion becomes increasingly sound. Again we come back to the proposition that in most business combinations in which the constituents are dealing at an arm's length the evidence appears to support a conclusion that the transaction has substance. Any aspects of the transaction which involve a disruption or modification of previously existing equities lend strength to the conclusion that a substantive change has arisen.

A fairly strong practical argument could likely be made to support pooling accounting in situations in which the cash outlay portion of the transaction is relatively minor. Any attempt to set a limit for the maximum cash transfer which could be made and not upset the suitability of pooling accounting would likely prove as fruitless as the past attempts to distinguish between combinations on the basis of relative size of the constituents. However, if a small portion of cash is involved and the conclusion is reached that this fact is insignificant from a substantive point of view, we feel total pooling accounting would be preferable to a part-purchase part-pooling approach. It appears to be particularly difficult to support a division of a combination transaction into two diverse pieces. Either an exchange took place or it did not take place, and contending that the transaction was partly an exchange and partly not an exchange is contradictory.

Multi-step combinations. Some combinations may be effected in which it appears that a part-purchase and part-pooling treatment is appropriate. However, closer examination will indicate that the purported "pooling" phase of the accounting treatment is in reality an extension of purchase accounting. For example, consider the situation in which Co. A acquired a 40% interest in Co. B in 1952 and accounted for this acquisition as a purchase. In subsequent years Co. A has reflected in its investment account its share of changes in Co. B's shareholders' equity. Several years later Co. A acquires all or a portion of the remaining 60% interest in Co. B by an exchange of stock. Proper accounting for this transaction would appear to be to account for the portion of the assets acquired in the latter exchange at their fair value at the date of the exchange and to continue to account for its share of Co. B presently owned at its equity in Co. B at that date. This equity is composed of its original cost adjusted for Co. A's share of changes in B's equity since acquisition. While this accounting for the 40% share of the interest may appear to be an application of pooling accounting, it is in reality a continuance of the existing basis for the investment held. An adjustment of this basis as of the date of acquisition of the remaining 60% would be appropriate, however, if evidence existed to indicate that previous accounting practices of Co. B had been inappropriate and had resulted in improper determinations of profits.

Another example is the situation in which one of the constituents in a 50%-owned company acquires the remaining 50% by an exchange of stock. Many 50%-owned companies are formed by the original constituents, so that the equity of each constituent in the joint venture is reflected in the investment account which may be adjusted periodically to reflect the change in book value of the jointly owned company. Thus, at the date of combination the acquiring company may be carrying its 50% investment at book value of the net assets represented by its 50% ownership. The fair value of the other 50% acquired would likely be different from the book value at the date of combination. In a combination of this type it appears that the 50% acquired should be accounted for at the fair value of that which is acquired, while the 50% formerly held should be carried forward at the equity at which it is carried. The result would be a part-purchase for the portion acquired in the exchange transaction and appear to be a part-pooling for the portion previously owned and as to which nothing of substance occurred in the transaction. This accounting for the portion previously owned, however, is in reality an extension of purchase accounting, and only the fact that the end result is similar to that which would exist through application of pooling accounting suggests that pooling accounting is applicable.

Part preferred shares and part common shares. The early views on pooling accounting limited its application basically to combinations in which common stock was the sole exchange medium. More recently a number of combinations have been consummated in which both preferred and common stock, or preferred only, have been used. A number of these combinations have been accounted for as poolings of interests. Some question has been raised as to the justification for this accounting treatment.

Once again we come back to our basic conclusion that proper accounting for a business combination depends far more on the basic nature of the transaction than on the vehicle by which it is accomplished. If the conclusion is reached that the transaction is principally one of form, without substance, as far as the accounting entity is concerned, a strong case can be made for pooling accounting. As noted in the cash discussion above, when exchange media other than cash are used in the transaction it appears to be more difficult to contend that substance is lacking. This would certainly appear to be the case if the preferred stock were cumulative and had specified rights as to liquidation. However, if convertible preferred were used, and if its other covenants indicated it was a mere substitute for common, one might be able to contend with some justification that the transaction was one of form and that pooling accounting would be appropriate.

Our view is that the use of any media other than common stock to effect an arm's-length combination is strong evidence that an exchange transaction of substance has occurred. Thus, the use of all preferred or part preferred and part common would usually indicate that purchase accounting is appropriate. The part-purchase, part-pooling accounting treatment sometimes suggested for this type of situation does not appear to have any applicability.

Minority interests. Until issuance of *Accounting Research Bulletin No. 48*, it did not appear to be proper to apply pooling accounting if the acquired company retained its identity as a subsidiary, and particularly would this be true if a minority interest remained in existence after the combination. *ARB No. 48* gave approval to the use of pooling accounting for combinations in which a subsidiary would remain in existence and also approved pooling accounting if an insignificant minority interest remained in existence.

If a combination would otherwise qualify for pooling accounting, as discussed above, we find nothing inherent in the subsidiary relationship to deny the use of pooling accounting. The existence of the acquired company as a subsidiary, a division, or a part of the legal parent without separate identification appears to be principally a matter of form.

The existence of a minority interest subsequent to the combination does appear to be a phenomenon of substance, however. The minority interest results because some of the owners of the acquired company did not want to merge or sell out, or for some other reason did not participate in the transaction. The transaction bears the earmarks of a purchase, an exchange, wherein one entity buys out the rights of some of the shareholders of a different entity, regardless of the device used to effect the transaction. The two entities have not, as units, pooled their interests.

Some may reason, on the other hand, that an insignificant minority remaining should not disqualify an otherwise pooling situation from pooling accounting. If this type of situation should arise, it would appear as if the accounting for the minority interest should be handled just as it would be in a normal parent-subsidiary situation. For the minority interest to exist, the subsidiary would remain in existence and its records would reflect its profits, etc. The parent company would presumably show in its investment account the book value of the assets acquired, adjusted each period for its share of the increase or decrease in the subsidiary's equity. The minority interest's share would be reported as a part of the minority interest.

The various problems discussed in this section are difficult to analyze on a logical basis principally because they arise from situations in which pooling accounting does not appear to be logically supportable. If the pooling accounting treatment were not extended to situations in which its application is questionable at best, a good many of the problems created by pooling accounting would never arise.

9

Conclusions and Recommendations

From the discussion in the preceding chapters certain generalizations can be made:

1. Business combinations have increased in frequency in recent years.

2. Business combinations have been effected in a number of different ways — through the use of assets, use of debt instruments, use of ownership equities.

3. Business combinations effected through the use of assets and debt instruments have been accounted for regularly under the purchase concept. That is, the assets or properties over which control is assumed are recorded on the basis of the cash or cash equivalent value of the assets given in exchange or liabilities assumed.

4. Business combinations effected through the use of ownership equities became increasingly common during the 1950's. The accounting treatment accorded such combinations grew gradually less well defined during this period, until by 1960 either of two acceptable alternative accounting treatments could be used to reflect a given combination.

5. The alternative accounting treatments in this area may produce widely varying results for the asset values recorded and the equity values carried forward into subsequent financial statements.

6. The concept of one of the alternatives, "pooling-of-interests ac-

CHAPTER 9: CONCLUSIONS AND RECOMMENDATIONS

counting," changed significantly during this period, so that by 1960 many combinations recorded as poolings bore little resemblance to the poolings of earlier years.

This existence of alternative accounting treatments, each possessing the stamp of general acceptability, and the application of the pooling treatment to combinations in which its propriety was questioned gave rise to the need for a thorough review of the area.

Conclusions

1. A business combination is an economic event of some importance. It is basically an exchange event in which two economic interests bargain to the consummation of an exchange of assets and/or equities.

2. Some business combinations have been viewed as exchanges and have been accounted for in a manner similar to that for other exchanges, i.e., the assets acquired were accounted for at the fair value of the consideration given or the fair value of the assets acquired.

3. Some business combinations have been viewed as exchanges without substance and have been accounted for in a manner which would retain as closely as possible the existing bases of accountability which the formerly separate entities had maintained.

4. Substantially all business combinations presently being consummated are exchange transactions between independent parties and involve a transference of assets. Proper accounting for this transfer is a basic aim of the accounting action to reflect business combinations.

5. At the present time many business combinations are being accounted for as poolings of interests even though the facts surrounding the transaction do not meet the criteria set forth in *Accounting Research Bulletin No. 48*, "Business Combinations."

6. The criteria set forth in *Accounting Research Bulletin No. 48* are artificial guidelines and fail to provide substantive clues to the nature of the combination transaction.

7. The growth of the existing pooling-of-interests concept was fostered by various forces, including several which have their base in accounting:

a. A hesitancy to recognize goodwill (excess of cost over book value of assets acquired), conditioned principally by the policy on amortization of goodwill as expressed in *Accounting Research Bulletin No. 43,* Chapter 5, provided impetus to acceptance of pooling accounting.

b. The growing importance attached to earnings per share by the business community and the pressure on managements to maintain or increase earnings per share on a year-to-year basis provided impetus to acceptance of pooling accounting.

c. The disparity between business earnings and taxable income which would result from accounting for most "tax-free" exchanges as purchases strengthened acceptance of pooling accounting.

8. The effect on earnings per share which will flow from the accounting for business combinations should not influence the accounting for business combinations.

Recommendations

1. A business combination which is basically an exchange transaction between independent parties should be accounted for in a manner similar to other exchange transactions.

a. The assets acquired should be accounted for at the fair value of the consideration given or the fair value of the assets received, whichever is more accurately determinable. This value is commonly described as the cost, exchange-price, or purchase-price.

b. The retained earnings of the resultant entity should be limited to the retained earnings of the acquiring company prior to combination, less adjustments coincident to the combination transaction. Any difference between the fair value of the assets acquired and the par or stated value of the shares given should be classified as paid-in surplus.

c. No basis exists in principle for a continuation of what is presently known as "pooling-of-interests" accounting *if* the business combination involves an exchange of assets and/or equities between independent parties.

2. A business combination in which no substantive changes occur, as in a combination between two legally separate but formerly related

entities, should be accounted for in a manner to retain as closely as possible the existing bases of accountability which the formerly separate entities had maintained.

   a. The asset bases existing on the records of the predecessor entities should be carried forward to the records of the resultant entity.
   b. The equity accounts of the predecessor entities should be carried forward to the resultant entity, except for adjustments necessitated by differences in par or stated value of the capital stock accounts or any other adjustments deemed necessary at the date of the combination.
   c. Adjustments of the accounting records which would otherwise be appropriate in the absence of the combination event are as important to recognize as if the combination had not occurred.

3. Any excess of fair value of assets acquired over their book value should be accounted for in the following manner:

   a. Any portion of the excess which is attributable to tangible assets or specific intangibles should be so allocated and should be amortized over the appropriate period of useful life.
   b. Any portion attributable to goodwill which appears to have limited value should be amortized over the period of expected limited life.
   c. Any portion attributable to goodwill which does not appear to have limited life should be carried forward to future periods until evidence exists that the value is impaired.

4. The determination of fair value of assets acquired in a business combination involving an exchange should be based upon a thorough consideration of all aspects of the negotiations. Market value of the shares transferred is only one of several possible determinants of fair value.

5. Normally, the existence of an exchange medium other than common shares in a business combination or the existence of a minority interest subsequent to a business combination should be presumptive evidence that the combination involved is an exchange transaction of substance and will be strongly indicative of the applicability of purchase accounting.

6. If the retained earnings of the resultant entity in a business combination are materially different from the earned surplus from a legal point of view, the earnings available for dividends should be disclosed in the financial statements.

7. As the constituents in business combinations approximate each other in terms of relative size it may be difficult to determine which constituent, in fact, acquires the other. Likewise, the resultant entity in such a combination is generally materially different in size, scope of operations, and earning potential from either constituent. When these conditions exist it may be appropriate to recognize the combination transaction as the basis for a "fresh start" in accounting for assets of each constituent.

   a. The assets of the resultant enterprise should be accounted for at their fair value at the date of the combination, as determined principally by review of the negotiations coincident to the exchange transaction.
   b. The resultant entity should not begin operations with any earned surplus because the enterprise is a new entity. However, in some circumstances, as when the law might require it or when regulatory reporting might require it, it may be appropriate for the resultant entity to report as earned surplus that amount which is legally available for dividends.
   c. In order to distinguish this concept of accounting for certain business combinations from the "pooling" concept widely followed today, we recommend that it be known as the "fair-value pooling" concept.

8. The "fair-value pooling" concept is applicable *only* when the facts of the transaction indicate clearly that the resultant entity is, in effect, a new enterprise. Considering business combinations in the mass, we would expect fair-value pooling to have limited application and would expect purchase accounting as outlined in item (1) of this section to be far more widely applicable.

9. Business combinations are significant events in the lives of most entities. Therefore, the facts of each business combination which produces a material change in the entity's financial statements should be disclosed. Likewise, the accounting treatment accorded the transaction should be disclosed. No restatement of prior years' financial statements appears necessary if the combination transaction is ac-

counted for as an exchange transaction. Fair-value poolings, on the other hand, represent a "fresh start." Therefore, comparisons of financial data subsequent to the "fresh start" with similar data prior to this event may not be meaningful. While restatement of previously presented financial data may be appropriate in some cases, it is preferable to eliminate the presentation for comparative purposes of financial data for periods prior to the "fresh start."

Another Look at Business Combinations*

A business combination occurs whenever two or more companies are brought together or combined under common ownership for the purpose of continuing to carry on the previously conducted businesses. The methods used to accomplish the combination determine whether it is to be deemed a purchase or a pooling of interests. Such determination, made at the time the combination takes place, can and probably will affect the net income reported by the enterprise for years to come.

One method by which a business combination may be brought about is by purchase in which an important part of the ownership interests are eliminated. In a combination of this type, one company (Company A) acquires control of the assets of another company (Company B) in exchange for cash or any other consideration except an equity interest in Company A. Examples of this type of acquisition are the purchase by Company A for cash of the net assets of Company B, and the purchase by Company A for cash of the outstanding shares of stock of Company B. In both examples the former shareholders in Company B have given up their ownership interests in the assets formerly owned and have no stake whatever in Company A.

Another method by which a business combination may be brought about is by a pooling of interests in which the ownership interests are combined. In a combination of this type, the stockholders of Company A and of Company B combine the net assets in which they have an ownership interest by exchanging shares of A for those of B, or by exchanging shares of B for those of A, or by forming a new company, C, to issue its shares for those of A and B. Upon completion of the

---

* This section was prepared by Robert C. Holsen, CPA, of Cleveland, Ohio, at the request of the Director of Accounting Research of the American Institute of CPAs.

exchange of shares a parent-subsidiary relationship has been created: that is, Company A is the parent and Company B is the subsidiary, or Company B is the parent and Company A is the subsidiary, or Company C is the parent and Company A and Company B are the subsidiaries. The transaction can end at this point or the parent can dissolve its subsidiary and absorb the subsidiary's assets into its own corporate structure. In another combination of this type, Company A exchanges its shares for the net assets of Company B and the latter liquidates, or Company B exchanges its shares for the net assets of Company A and the latter liquidates, or a new company, C, exchanges its shares for the net assets of A and B and the latter liquidate. The effect of each of these alternatives is the same; in each case nothing has been taken from the combination of Company A plus Company B, nothing has been added to it, and the shareholders of both Company A and Company B have maintained their ownership interests.

In chapter 7, page 69, Arthur Wyatt states that "a business combination occurs when one company acquires, assumes, or otherwise gains control over the assets... of another company by an exchange of assets or equities...." Instead of being a definition of all business combinations, this is a definition of a purchase, a particular kind of business combination. In a purchase one company does acquire control over the assets of another, but that does not hold true in a pooling of interests. In a pooling, one company does not acquire the assets or control of another; rather the shareholders who controlled one company join with the shareholders who controlled the other company to form the combined group of shareholders who control the combined companies.

From these comments are drawn the following conclusions:

1. A purchase occurs when consideration other than equity shares is exchanged and one group of shareholders gives up its ownership interest in the assets it formerly controlled.

2. A pooling of interests occurs when equity shares are exchanged and both groups of shareholders continue their ownership interests in the combined companies.

3. As Arthur Wyatt has demonstrated, criteria such as relative size and continuity of management, as set forth in *Accounting Research Bulletin No. 48,* cannot be supported by logic; certainly they have not been followed in practice.

If the factors involved indicate that the combination qualifies as a pooling, it should be treated as a pooling and not as a purchase. Paragraph 8 of *ARB No. 48* describes the accounting treatment to be afforded a purchase; paragraphs 9 through 12 of the same bulletin set forth the accounting considerations applicable to a pooling of interests. Some state laws do not at the present time explicitly provide for the pooling-of-interests treatment. If otherwise appropriate, however, this treatment should be used in the financial statements and the situation suitably disclosed.

So far the remarks relating to a pooling of interests have not defined what is meant by an exchange of shares. In its purest and strictest sense the "exchange of shares" envisages the exchange of unissued shares of common stock of one company for all of the outstanding shares of common stock of another company. However, the recent history of business combinations has furnished many cases in which poolings were consummated by methods which did not meet the strict test of the above definition. These other methods have involved the use of cash and common stock, common and preferred stock, preferred stock alone, and treasury stock of the one company for all of the outstanding common stock of another or for most of the outstanding stock with a few shares remaining as a minority interest. Whether these alternatives can be deemed to be acceptable methods for considering a business combination to be in fact a pooling of interests is discussed in the following paragraphs.

Beginning on page 99, Arthur Wyatt presents an excellent discourse on business combinations involving the use of cash and common stock. As he says, "it is difficult to contend that nothing of substance has occurred in the transaction" when cash is part of the consideration. From a practical standpoint, however, the use of a small amount of cash (e.g., in lieu of issuing fractional shares or for payments to dissenters) should not deny the companies the right to consider the transaction a pooling. The problem arises in setting a maximum limit on the "small amount of cash." Perhaps the solution to the problem could be found in relating the amount of cash involved to the entire transaction; if the amount of cash is not material in relation to the transaction, the combination should be considered to be a pooling of interests; conversely, if the amount of cash involved is material, the transaction should be considered to be a purchase.

Issuance of preferred stock of one company for the common stock of another in a business combination provides other complications for determining whether such a transaction can be treated as a pooling of interests. When the preferred stock is nonvoting, it would seem apparent that one group of shareowners has relinquished a substantial share of its ownership interests and, accordingly, a transaction involving nonvoting preferred stock must be a purchase. When preferred stocks are redeemable, either at the option of the company or in accordance with a schedule arranged at the time of their issuance, the preferred stockholders lose their ownership interests, and the original exchange of the redeemable preferred stock for common stock also is a purchase. Even when preferred stocks have voting rights and are not redeemable, the transaction should be treated as a purchase, because, by its very nature, preferred stock is different from common stock in that the former generally has specific rights in liquidation and a prior position with respect to sharing in the earnings. By accepting preferred stock for the common stock previously held, the preferred shareholders have surrendered a portion of their ownership interests for a preferred position in the combined companies, and the status of the former common shareholders in one company does not remain the same after they accept preferred stock of the combined company. Accordingly, the issuance of preferred stock of one company for common stock of another should result in the business combination being treated as a purchase. One exception would occur when the preferred stock is convertible into common and the terms of its issuance indicate that it is basically only a substitute for common stock; use of such convertible preferred stock should allow the combination to be treated as a pooling of interests. Another exception should be allowed when the combination involves the issuance of both common and preferred stocks but the preferred stock is not material in relation to the entire transaction.

The use of treasury stock in a business combination also raises questions as to whether the transaction is a purchase or a pooling. There have been a number of instances in which treasury stock acquired after the commencement of negotiations relating to the combination has been used to consummate a pooling. In fact, some listing applications filed with the New York Stock Exchange refer to the use of treasury stock to be acquired after the date of the listing application. In other cases treasury stock acquired prior to the commencement of negotiations has been used. The exchange of treasury stock specifically acquired for use in a business combination to be effected in a short period of time after acquisition of the treasury stock should make the transaction a purchase since the net assets of the combined companies would be reduced. While this method may have certain tax advantages, the result, insofar as the business combination is concerned, is the same as the use of cash. There may be times when evidence proves that the treasury stock has been acquired solely for use in a business combination, but generally there is a serious question as to whether the stock has been acquired for that purpose. The answer hinges on motivation and intent, which are not subject to objective determination. A rule based upon the length of time the stock is held in the treasury might provide a solution, except that any time period selected would, of necessity, be arbitrary and subject to the same type of erosion that was applied to the concept of size of the constituent companies as enunciated in paragraph 6 of *ARB No. 48*. A better guide might be found by referring to the earlier comments about the maintenance by the shareholders of the constituent companies of their ownership interests in the combined enterprise. Elimination of a material portion of the shareholders' interest by acquiring their stock for the treasury or immediately prior to the occurrence of the business combination should make the transaction a purchase.

Subsequent to the issuance of *ARB No. 48* permitting a pooling with "the continuance in existence of one or more of the constituent corporations in a subsidiary relationship," minority interests have emerged in business combinations deemed to be poolings. There should be no question as to the propriety of the appearance of this minority. A small portion of shareholders who, for their own reasons, do not care to participate in the merger should not deny the transaction the right to be treated as a pooling if it otherwise so qualifies. Here again the problem involves setting the maximum limit on the acceptable size of the minority interest and the answer is found in the concept that in a pooling the shareholders of the constituent companies continue in the combined enterprise. A reasonable guide would be the relation of the size of the minority interest to the subsidiary company. If the minority interest is not material in relation to the subsidiary company, the transaction should be treated as a pooling while, if the minority interest is material in relation to the subsidiary, the transaction should be considered to be a purchase.

One of the usual consequences of treating a business combination as a purchase is the creation of an intangible asset, often called goodwill, representing the excess of purchase cost over the fair value of the assets acquired. These acquired assets would include tangible assets as well as, in many cases, such identifiable intangibles as patents, licenses, copyrights, specific sales contracts, and the like.

The accounting treatment afforded the goodwill created in the purchase seldom is satisfactory. If the goodwill is not amortized, it remains in the balance sheet as an asset to be considered, in most cases, as a necessary evil. Some measure of the importance attached to goodwill can be gathered from a quotation from an article in the December, 1961, issue of *The Banking Law Journal* by Homer Kripke who notes that "the loss of goodwill as a balance sheet asset is deemed of no importance, because accountants and financial analysts have come to regard such intangibles with suspicion and to automatically disregard them in computing net worth. Lawyers, following the same lead, frequently require the exclusion of intangibles in the definitions controlling the computation of net worth and of balance sheet ratios in indenture restrictions." If, on the other hand, the goodwill is amortized by charges to income, the amortization period selected usually is arbitrary and bears no relation to any demonstrable diminution in the value of this intangible asset.

Accordingly, it is suggested that the accounting policy with respect to the write-off of goodwill should be re-examined and consideration given to allowing a company to charge to earned surplus the amount of goodwill at the date of its acquisition.

APPENDIX

Accounting Research BULLETINS
★
Issued by the
Committee on Accounting Procedure,
American Institute of Accountants,
13 East 41st Street, New York 17, N. Y.
Copyright 1944 by American Institute of Accountants

December, 1944

NO. 24

Accounting for Intangible Assets

This bulletin deals with some of the problems involved in accounting for certain types of assets classified by accountants as intangibles, including those acquired by the issuance of securities as well as those purchased for cash. Such assets may be purchased or acquired separately at a specified price or consideration, or may be purchased or acquired, together with other assets, for a lump-sum price or consideration, without specification by either the seller or the purchaser at the time of purchase, of the portion of the total price which is applicable to the respective assets thus acquired. The bulletin does not deal with the problems of accounting for intangibles developed in the regular course of business by research, experimentation, advertising, or otherwise.

The intangibles herein considered may be broadly classified as follows:

> (a) Those having a term of existence limited by law, regulation, or agreement, or by their nature (such as patents, copyrights, leases, licenses, franchises for a fixed term, and goodwill as to which there is evidence of limited duration).
>
> (b) Those having no such limited term of existence and as to which there is, at the time of acquisition, no indication of limited

---

[1] Other problems arising from partial loss of value of type (b) intangibles are not dealt with herein. See discussion, page 120.

life (such as goodwill generally, going value, trade names, secret processes, subscription lists, perpetual franchises, and organization costs).

(c) The excess of a parent company's investment in the stock of a subsidiary over its equity in the net assets of the subsidiary as shown by the latter's books at the date of acquisition, in so far as that excess would be treated as an intangible in consolidated financial statements of the parent and the subsidiary. This class of asset may represent intangibles of either type (a) or type (b) above or a combination of both.

The intangibles described above will hereinafter be referred to as type (a) and (b) intangibles, respectively.

Summary Statement

(1) The initial carrying value of all types of intangibles should be cost, in accordance with the generally accepted accounting principle that assets should be stated at cost when they are acquired. In the case of noncash acquisitions, cost may be determined either by the fair value of the consideration given or by the fair value of the property acquired, whichever is the more clearly evident.

(2) The cost of type (a) intangibles should be amortized by systematic charges in the income statement over the period benefited, as in the case of other assets having a limited period of usefulness.

(3) The cost of type (b) intangibles may be carried continuously unless and until it becomes reasonably evident that the term of existence of such intangibles has become limited, or that they have become worthless. In the former event the cost should be amortized by systematic charges in the income statement over the estimated remaining period of usefulness or, if such charges would result in distortion of the income statement, a partial write-down may be made by a charge to earned surplus, and the balance of the cost may be amortized over the remaining period of usefulness. If an investment in type (b) intangibles is determined to have become worthless, the carrying value should be charged off either in the income statement or to earned surplus as, in the circumstances, may be appropriate.[1] In determining whether an investment in type (b) intangibles has become, or is likely to become worthless, it is proper to take into account any new and related elements of intangible value, acquired or developed, which have replaced or become merged with such intangibles.

(4) Where a corporation decides that a type (b) intangible may

not continue to have value during the entire life of the enterprise, it may amortize the cost of such intangible despite the fact that there are no present indications of such limited life which would require reclassification as type (a), and despite the fact that expenditures are being made to maintain its value. In such cases the cost may be amortized over a reasonable period of time, by systematic charges in the income statement. The procedure should be formally approved, preferably by action of the stockholders, and the facts should be fully disclosed in the financial statements. Such amortization is within the discretion of the corporation and is not to be regarded as obligatory.

(5) There is a presumption, when the price paid for a stock investment in a subsidiary is greater than the net assets of such subsidiary applicable thereto, as carried on its books at date of acquisition, that the parent company, in effect, placed a value greater than book value on some of the assets of the subsidiary in arriving at the price it was willing to pay for its investment therein. If practicable there should be an allocation of such excess as between tangible and intangible property and any amount allocated to intangibles should be further allocated to determine a separate cost for each type (a) intangible and for at least the aggregate of all type (b) intangibles. The amounts so allocated to intangibles should thereafter be dealt with in accordance with paragraphs (1), (2), (3), and (4) hereof.

(6) In connection with the foregoing procedures, the committee recognizes that in the past it has been accepted practice to eliminate type (b) intangibles by writing them off against any existing surplus, capital or earned, even though the value of the asset is unimpaired. Since the practice has been long established and widely approved, the committee does not feel warranted in recommending, at this time, adoption of a rule prohibiting such disposition. The committee believes, however, that such dispositions should be discouraged, especially if proposed to be effected by charges to capital surplus.

Discussion

In dealing with the intangible assets herein considered, important questions arise as to the initial carrying value of such assets, the amortization of carrying value where their term of existence is definitely limited or problematical, and the adjustment of carrying value where there is a substantial and permanent decline in the value of such assets. These questions involve basic accounting principles of balance-sheet presentation and income determination. The committee believes that the accounting for intangibles has heretofore been regarded as being of relatively minor importance; accounting practices with respect thereto have varied greatly. The present bulletin is designed to promote a fuller consideration of the relation of intangibles to income and earned surplus.

Initial carrying value. The committee has heretofore taken the position that the accounting for tangible fixed assets should normally be based on cost,[2] which may be defined generally as the price paid or consideration given to acquire the asset in question. Attention is now directed to the fact that the same principle is applicable to intangibles.

The committee has considered two further problems which may arise in the determination of the cost of intangibles. Since intangibles are frequently acquired in exchange for securities, the committee points out that in the case of noncash acquisitions cost may be determined either by the fair value of the consideration given or by the fair value of the property acquired, whichever is the more clearly evident.

The second problem arises in cases where a group of intangibles or a mixed aggregate of tangible and intangible property is acquired for a lump-sum price or consideration. It is essential in such cases that an allocation of the aggregate cost be made as between tangible and intangible property, and it is manifestly desirable that the cost of intangibles be further allocated to determine a separate cost for each type (a) intangible so acquired and for the aggregate, at least, of all type (b) intangibles.

Amortization accounting. The cost of tangible assets having a limited term of usefulness is dealt with by depreciation accounting, which the committee on terminology has defined as a system of amortization which aims to distribute the cost or other basic value of tangible capital assets, less salvage value (if any), over the estimated useful life of the unit (which may be a group of assets) in a rational manner.[3] In like manner the cost of intangible assets having a limited term of usefulness should be dealt with under amortization accounting. To this end the committee has classified intangibles as between type (a) which includes those having a term of existence limited by law, regulation, or agreement, or by their nature; and type (b) which includes those as to which there is, at the time of acquisition, no evidence of

---

[2] *Accounting Research Bulletin No. 5.*
[3] *Accounting Research Bulletin No. 22.*

limited life. The committee recognizes that there may be cases in which it is difficult to make such a classification.

The cost of intangibles classified as type (a) should be amortized by systematic charges in the income statement over the period benefited. If it becomes evident that the period benefited will be longer or shorter than originally estimated, recognition thereof may take the form of an appropriate decrease or increase in the rate of amortization or if such increased charges would result in distortion of the income statement a partial write-down may be made by a charge to earned surplus.

The intangibles classified as type (b) may be carried continuously at cost unless and until it becomes reasonably evident that their term of existence has become limited, or that they have become worthless. In the former event they should be reclassified as type (a) and thereafter amortized by systematic charges in the income statement over the estimated remaining period of usefulness. If that period of amortization is relatively short so that misleading inferences might be drawn as a result of the inclusion of substantial charges in the income statement, a partial write-down may be made by a charge to earned surplus and the balance of the cost may be amortized over the remaining period of usefulness.

In the event of complete loss of an investment in type (b) intangibles, a charge should be made either in the income statement or to earned surplus as, in the circumstances, may be appropriate.

In determining whether an investment in type (b) intangibles has or is likely to become worthless, consideration should be given to the fact that in some cases intangibles acquired by purchase may merge with, or be replaced by, intangibles acquired or developed with respect to other products or lines of business, and that in such circumstances the discontinuance of a product or line of business may not in fact indicate loss of value.

Partial loss of value. The committee recognizes that changes in general economic conditions and changes affecting the business of a particular company may have an important effect on the value, at a given time, of its intangibles. It further recognizes the difficulty of determining whether adverse changes are temporary or permanent. The problems arising as a result of such partial loss of value (as contrasted with total loss of value discussed above), which are also applicable to tangible assets (such as, loss of commercial value of tangible capital assets not covered by depreciation accounting), are not dealt with herein but are in their broader aspects presently under consideration by the committee. Attention is drawn however, to Rule No. 2, adopted by the membership of the Institute in 1934, which provides that "capital surplus, however created, should not be used to relieve the income account of the current or future years of charges that would otherwise fall to be made thereagainst." [4]

Discretionary amortization of intangibles. If a corporation decides to amortize the cost of a type (b) intangible, as to which there is no present indication of limited existence or loss of value, by systematic charges in the income statement, such procedure is permissible despite the fact that expenditures are being made to maintain its value. The plan of amortization should be reasonable; it should be based on all the surrounding circumstances including the basic nature of the intangible and the expenditures being currently made for development, experimentation, and sales promotion. Where the intangibles are important income-producing factors and are being currently maintained by advertising or otherwise, the period of amortization should be reasonably long. The procedure should be formally approved, preferably by action of the stockholders, and should be fully disclosed in the financial statements. The committee believes that such amortization should be entirely within the discretion of the corporation and should not be regarded as mandatory.

Intangibles in consolidation. Where a parent corporation has made a stock investment in a subsidiary, at a cost in excess of its equity in the net assets of the subsidiary as shown by its books at the date of acquisition, the parent corporation may have (a) paid amounts in excess of book value for specific assets of the subsidiary or (b) paid for the general goodwill of the subsidiary. If practicable, such an excess should be divided as between tangible and intangible assets, and the amount allocated to intangibles should be further allocated as between each type (a) intangible and the aggregate, at least, of all type (b) intangibles. The amounts so allocated should thereafter be dealt with in accordance with the rules hereinbefore set forth.

Write-off where there is no evidence of loss of value. In adopting the procedures set forth above the committee recognizes that in the past it has generally been considered proper to eliminate the cost of type

---

[4] *Accounting Research Bulletin No. 1,* p. 6.

(b) intangibles from the accounts, in whole or in part, by a charge against any existing surplus, capital or earned, even though the value of the asset is unimpaired. Since the practice has been long established and widely approved, the committee does not feel warranted in recommending, at this time, adoption of a rule prohibiting such disposition. In addition the matter of charges to capital surplus requires further consideration and is part of the general problem of surplus accounting on the study of which the committee is presently engaged.

The committee believes, however, that such dispositions should be discouraged, especially if proposed to be effected by charges to capital surplus. It points out that the reduction of the investment, upon which the responsibility and accountability of management is based, may give rise to misleading inferences if subsequent earnings are compared with the reduced base.

Accounting for Intangible Assets

The statement entitled "Accounting for Intangible Assets" was adopted by the assenting votes of eighteen members of the committee, as it was constituted at the time of the 1944 annual meeting of the Institute. Mr. Willcox dissented. Mr. Stans dissented from paragraph (5) of the summary statement and the related discussion. Mr. Zebley dissented from paragraphs (5) and (6) of the summary statement and the related discussion

Notes

1. Accounting Research Bulletins represent the considered opinion of at least two-thirds of the members of the committee on accounting procedure, reached on a formal vote after examination of the subject matter by the committee and the research department. Except in cases in which formal adoption by the Institute membership has been asked and secured, the authority of the bulletins rests upon the general acceptability of opinions so reached. (See Report of Committee on Accounting Procedure to Council, dated September 18, 1939.)

2. Recommendations of the committee are not intended to be retroactive, nor applicable to immaterial items. (See Bulletin No. 1, page 3.)

3. It is recognized also that any general rules may be subject to exception; it is felt, however, that the burden of justifying departure from accepted procedures must be assumed by those who adopt other treatment. (See Bulletin No. 1, page 3).

COMMITTEE ON ACCOUNTING PROCEDURE (1943-1944)

WALTER A. STAUB, *(Chairman)*	ANSON HERRICK	JACKSON W. SMART
GEORGE D. BAILEY	HENRY A. HORNE	MAURICE H. STANS
WILLIAM H. BELL	PAUL K. KNIGHT	CHARLES H. TOWNS
ARCHIBALD BOWMAN	GEORGE O. MAY	R. S. WILLCOX
GEORGE COCHRANE	WARREN W. NISSLEY	JOHN H. ZEBLEY, JR.
CHARLES B. COUCHMAN	WILLIAM A. PATON	
WILLIAM D. CRANSTOUN	MAURICE E. PELOUBET	JAMES L. DOHR,
STEPHEN GILMAN	HIRAM T. SCOVILL	*Director of Research*

Accounting Research BULLETINS

★

Issued by the
Committee on Accounting Procedure,
American Institute of Accountants,
270 Madison Avenue, New York 16, N. Y.
Copyright 1950 by American Institute of Accountants

September, 1950

NO. 40

Business Combinations

1. Whenever two or more corporations are brought together, or combined, for the purpose of carrying on in a single corporation the previously conducted businesses, the accounting to give effect to the combination will vary depending upon whether there is a continuance of the former ownership or a new ownership.[1] This statement has been prepared (a) for the purpose of differentiating between these two types of corporate combinations, the first of which is designated herein as a *pooling of interests* and the second as a *purchase*, and (b) to indicate the nature of the accounting treatment appropriate to each type.

2. For accounting purposes, the distinction between a pooling of interests and a purchase is to be found in the attendant circumstances rather than in the legal designation as a merger or a consolidation, or legal considerations with respect to availability of net assets for dividends, or provisions of the Internal Revenue Code with respect to income taxes. In a pooling of interests, all or substantially all of the equity interests in predecessor corporations continue, as such, in a surviving corporation [1] which may be one of the predecessor corpora-

---

[1] When the shares of stock in the surviving corporation that are received by the several owners of one of the predecessor companies are not substantially in proportion to their respective interests in the predecessor company, a new ownership or purchase of such company is presumed to result.

tions, or in a new one created for the purpose. In a purchase, on the other hand, part or all of the ownership of the acquired corporation is eliminated. A plan or firm intention and understanding to retire capital stock issued to the owners of one or more of the corporate parties, or substantial changes in ownership occurring immediately before or after the combination, would also tend to indicate that the combination is a purchase.

3. Other factors to be taken into consideration in determining whether a purchase or a pooling of interests is involved are the relative size of the constituent companies and the continuity of management or power to control the management. Thus, a purchase may be indicated when one corporate party to a combination is quite minor in size in relation to the others, or where the management of one of the corporate parties to the combination is eliminated or its influence upon the management of the surviving corporation is quite small. Other things being equal, the presumption that a pooling of interests is involved would be strengthened if the activities of the businesses to be combined are either similar or complementary. No one of these factors would necessarily be determinative, but their presence or absence would be cumulative in effect.

4. When a combination is deemed to be a purchase the assets purchased should be recorded on the books of the acquiring company at cost, measured in money or the fair value of other consideration given, or at the fair value of the property acquired, whichever is more clearly evident. This is in accordance with the procedure applicable to accounting for purchases of assets.

5. When a combination is deemed to be a pooling of interests, the necessity for a new basis of accountability does not arise. The book values of the assets of the constituent companies, when stated in conformity with generally accepted accounting principles and appropriately adjusted when deemed necessary to place them on a uniform basis, should be carried forward; and retained incomes of the constituent companies may be carried forward. If one party to such a combination had been acquired as a subsidiary by another such party prior to the origin of a plan of combination, the parent's share of the retained income of the subsidiary prior to such acquisition should not be included in the retained income account of the pooled companies.

6. Due to the variety of conditions under which a pooling of interests may be carried out it is not practicable to deal with the accounting

presentation except in general terms. A number of problems will arise. For example, the aggregate of stated capital of the surviving corporation in a pooling of interests may be either more than, or less than, the total of the stated capital of the predecessor corporations. In the former event the excess should be deducted first from the aggregate of any other contributed capital (capital surplus), and next from the aggregate of any retained income (earned surplus) of the predecessors; while in the latter event the difference should appear in the balance sheet of the surviving corporation as other contributed capital (capital surplus), analogous to that created by a reduction in stated capital where no combination is involved.

The statement entitled "Business Combinations" was unanimously adopted by the twenty-one members of the committee. Messrs. Andrews, Paton, and Wellington assented with qualification.

Messrs. Andrews, Paton, and Wellington qualify their assent because they believe paragraph 5 is misleading in so far as it fails to make clear that any adjustment of asset values or of retained income which would be in conformity with generally accepted accounting principles in the absence of a combination would be equally so if effected in connection with a pooling of interests.

Notes

1. Accounting Research Bulletins represent the considered opinion of at least two-thirds of the members of the committee on accounting procedure, reached on a formal vote after examination of the subject matter by the committee and the research department. Except in cases in which formal adoption by the Institute membership has been asked and secured, the authority of the bulletins rests upon the general acceptability of opinions so reached. (See Report of Committee on Accounting Procedure to Council, dated September 18, 1939.)

2. Recommendations of the committee are not intended to be retroactive, nor applicable to immaterial items. (See Bulletin No. 1, page 3.)

3. It is recognized also that any general rules may be subject to exception; it is felt, however, that the burden of justifying departure from accepted procedures must be assumed by those who adopt other treatment. (See Bulletin No. 1, page 3.)

Committee on Accounting Procedure (1949-1950)

Samuel J. Broad,
   Chairman
Frederick B. Andrews
Frank S. Calkins
James L. Dohr
George P. Ellis
H. A. Finney
J. P. Friedman
Thomas G. Higgins

John B. Inglis
Paul K. Knight
John A. Lindquist
Edward J. McDevitt
Leslie Mills
William A. Paton
Maurice E. Peloubet
John W. Queenan
James A. Runser

Walter L. Schaffer
Virgil S. Tilly
C. Oliver Wellington
Edward B. Wilcox

───────────

Carman G. Blough
   Director of Research

Excerpt From *Accounting Research Bulletin No. 43*

Chapter 5: Intangible Assets

1. This chapter deals with problems involved in accounting for certain types of assets classified by accountants as intangibles, specifically those acquired by the issuance of securities or purchased for cash or other consideration. Such assets may be purchased or acquired separately for a specified consideration or may be purchased or acquired, together with other assets, for a lump-sum consideration without specification by either the seller or the purchaser, at the time of purchase, of the portions of the total price which are applicable to the respective assets thus acquired. In dealing with the intangible assets herein considered, important questions arise as to the initial carrying amount of such assets, the amortization of such amount where their term of existence is definitely limited or problematical, and their write-down or write-off at some later time where there is a substantial and permanent decline in the value of such assets. These questions involve basic accounting principles of balance sheet presentation and income determination and this chapter is designed to promote a fuller consideration of those principles. It does not, however, deal with the problems of accounting for intangibles developed in the regular course of business by research, experimentation, advertising, or otherwise.

Classification of Intangibles

2. The intangibles herein considered may be broadly classified as follows:

> (a) Those having a term of existence limited by law, regulation, or agreement, or by their nature (such as patents, copyrights, leases, licenses, franchises for a fixed term, and goodwill as to which there is evidence of limited duration);
>
> (b) Those having no such limited term of existence and as to

which there is, at the time of acquisition, no indication of limited life (such as goodwill generally, going value, trade names, secret processes, subscription lists, perpetual franchises, and organization costs).

3. The intangibles described above will hereinafter be referred to as type (a) and type (b) intangibles, respectively. The portion of a lump-sum consideration deemed to have been paid for intangible elements when a mixed aggregate of tangible and intangible property is acquired, or the excess of a parent company's investment in the stock of a subsidiary over its equity in the net assets of the subsidiary as shown by the latter's books at the date of acquisition, in so far as that excess would be treated as an intangible in consolidated financial statements of the parent and the subsidiary, may represent intangibles of either type (a) or type (b) or a combination of both.

Initial Carrying Amount

4. The initial amount assigned to all types of intangibles should be cost, in accordance with the generally accepted accounting principle that assets should be stated at cost when they are acquired. In the case of noncash acquisitions, as, for example, where intangibles are acquired in exchange for securities, cost may be considered as being either the fair value of the consideration given or the fair value of the property or right acquired, whichever is the more clearly evident.

Amortization of Intangibles

Type (a)

5. The cost of type (a) intangibles should be amortized by systematic charges in the income statement over the period benefited, as in the case of other assets having a limited period of usefulness. If it becomes evident that the period benefited will be longer or shorter than originally estimated, recognition thereof may take the form of an appropriate decrease or increase in the rate of amortization or, if such increased charges would result in distortion of income, a partial write-down may be made by a charge to earned surplus.

Type (b)

6. When it becomes reasonably evident that the term of existence of a type (b) intangible has become limited and that it has therefore become a type (a) intangible, its cost should be amortized by system-

atic charges in the income statement over the estimated remaining period of usefulness. If, however, the period of amortization is relatively short so that misleading inferences might be drawn as a result of inclusion of substantial charges in the income statement a partial write-down may be made by a charge to earned surplus,[1] and the rest of the cost may be amortized over the remaining period of usefulness.

7. When a corporation decides that a type (b) intangible may not continue to have value during the entire life of the enterprise it may amortize the cost of such intangible by systematic charges against income despite the fact that there are no present indications of limited existence or loss of value which would indicate that it has become type (a), and despite the fact that expenditures are being made to maintain its value. Such amortization is within the discretion of the company and is not to be regarded as obligatory. The plan of amortization should be reasonable; it should be based on all the surrounding circumstances, including the basic nature of the intangible and the expenditures currently being made for development, experimentation, and sales promotion. Where the intangible is an important income-producing factor and is currently being maintained by advertising or otherwise, the period of amortization should be reasonably long. The procedure should be formally approved and the reason for amortization, the rate used, and the shareholders' or directors' approval thereof should be disclosed in the financial statements.

Write-off of Intangibles

8. The cost of type (b) intangibles should be written off when it becomes reasonably evident that they have become worthless. Under such circumstances the amount at which they are carried on the books should be charged off in the income statement or, if the amount is so large that its effect on income may give rise to misleading inferences, it should be charged to earned surplus.[1] In determining whether an investment in type (b) intangibles has become or is likely to become worthless, consideration should be given to the fact that in some cases intangibles acquired by purchase may merge with, or be replaced by, intangibles acquired or developed with respect to other products or lines of business and that in such circumstances the discontinuance of a product or line of business may not in fact indicate loss of value.

---

[1] See chapter 8, paragraphs 11, 12, and 13.

Limitation on Write-off of Intangibles

9. Lump-sum write-offs of intangibles should not be made to earned surplus immediately after acquisition, nor should intangibles be charged against capital surplus. If not amortized systematically, intangibles should be carried at cost until an event has taken place which indicates a loss or a limitation on the useful life of the intangibles.

Purchase of Subsidiary's Stock or Basket Purchase of Assets

10. A problem arises in cases where a group of intangibles or a mixed aggregate of tangible and intangible property is acquired for a lump-sum consideration, or when the consideration given for a stock investment in a subsidiary is greater than the net assets of such subsidiary applicable thereto, as carried on its books at the date of acquisition. In this latter type of situation there is a presumption that the parent company, in effect, placed a valuation greater than their carrying amount on some of the assets of the subsidiary in arriving at the price it was willing to pay for its investment therein. The parent corporation may have (a) paid amounts in excess of carrying amounts for specific assets of the subsidiary or (b) paid for the general goodwill of the subsidiary. In these cases, if practicable, there should be an allocation, as between tangible and intangible property, of the cost of the mixed aggregate of property or of the excess of a parent's investment over its share of the amount at which the subsidiary carried its net assets on its books at the date of acquisition. Any amount allocated to intangibles should be further allocated to determine, if practicable, a separate cost for each type (a) intangible and for at least the aggregate of all type (b) intangibles. The amounts so allocated to intangibles should thereafter be dealt with in accordance with the procedures outlined in this chapter.

Excerpt From *Accounting Research Bulletin No. 43*

Chapter 7: Capital Accounts

SECTION C | *Business Combinations*

1. Whenever two or more corporations are brought together, or combined, for the purpose of carrying on in a single corporation the previously conducted businesses, the accounting to give effect to the combination will vary depending upon whether there is a continuance of the former ownership or a new ownership.[1] This section (a) differentiates these two types of corporate combinations, the first of which is designated herein as a *pooling of interests* and the second as a *purchase;* and (b) indicates the nature of the accounting treatment appropriate to each type.

2. For accounting purposes, the distinction between a pooling of interests and a purchase is to be found in the attendant circumstances rather than in the legal designation as a merger or a consolidation, or in legal considerations with respect to availability of net assets for dividends, or provisions of the Internal Revenue Code with respect to income taxes. In a pooling of interests, all or substantially all of the equity interests in predecessor corporations continue, as such, in a surviving corporation[1] which may be one of the predecessor corpora-

---

[1] When the shares of stock in the surviving corporation that are received by the several owners of one of the predecessor companies are not substantially in proportion to their respective interests in the predecessor company, a new ownership or purchase of such company is presumed to result.

tions, or in a new one created for the purpose. In a purchase, on the other hand, an important part or all of the ownership of the acquired corporation is eliminated. A plan or firm intention and understanding to retire capital stock issued to the owners of one or more of the corporate parties, or substantial changes in ownership occurring immediately before or after the combination, would also tend to indicate that the combination is a purchase.

3. Other factors to be taken into consideration in determining whether a purchase or a pooling of interests is involved are the relative size of the constituent companies and the continuity of management or power to control the management. Thus, a purchase may be indicated when one corporate party to a combination is quite minor in size in relation to the others, or where the management of one of the corporate parties to the combination is eliminated or its influence upon the management of the surviving corporation is very small. Other things being equal, the presumption that a pooling of interests is involved would be strengthened if the activities of the businesses to be combined are either similar or complementary. No one of these factors would necessarily be determinative, but their presence or absence would be cumulative in effect.

4. When a combination is deemed to be a purchase the assets purchased should be recorded on the books of the acquiring company at cost, measured in money or the fair value of other consideration given, or at the fair value of the property acquired, whichever is more clearly evident. This is in accordance with the procedure applicable to accounting for purchases of assets.

5. When a combination is deemed to be a pooling of interests, the necessity for a new basis of accountability does not arise. The carrying amounts of the assets of the constituent companies, if stated in conformity with generally accepted accounting principles and appropriately adjusted when deemed necessary to place them on a uniform basis, should be carried forward; and earned surpluses of the constituent companies may be carried forward. However, any adjustment of assets or of surplus which would be in conformity with generally accepted accounting principles in the absence of a combination would be equally so if effected in connection with a pooling of interests. If one party to such a combination had been acquired by purchase as a subsidiary by another such party prior to the origin of a plan of combination, the parent's share of the earned surplus of the subsidiary prior

to such acquisition should not be included in the earned surplus account of the pooled companies.

6. Because of the variety of conditions under which a pooling of interests may be carried out it is not practicable to deal with the accounting presentation except in general terms. A number of problems will arise. For example, the stated capital of the surviving corporation in a pooling of interests may be either more than, or less than, the total of the stated capital of the predecessor corporations. In the former event the excess should be deducted first from the total of any other contributed capital (capital surplus), and next from the total of any earned surplus of the predecessors, while in the latter event the difference should appear in the balance sheet of the surviving corporation as other contributed capital (capital surplus), analogous to that created by a reduction in stated capital where no combination is involved.

7. When a combination results in carrying forward the earned surpluses of the constituent companies, statements of operations issued by the continuing business for the period in which the combination occurs and for any preceding period should show the results of operations of the combined interests.

Accounting Research BULLETINS

★
Issued by the
Committee on Accounting Procedure,
American Institute of Accountants,
270 Madison Avenue, New York 16, N. Y.
Copyright 1957 by American Institute of Accountants

January, 1957

NO. 48

Business Combinations

(Supersedes chapter 7(c) of Accounting Research Bulletin No. 43)

1. Whenever two or more corporations are brought together, or combined, for the purpose of carrying on the previously conducted businesses, the accounting to give effect to the combination will vary depending largely upon whether an important part of the former ownership is eliminated or whether substantially all of it is continued. This bulletin differentiates these two types of combinations, the first of which is designated herein as a *purchase* and the second as a *pooling of interests*, and indicates the nature of the accounting treatment appropriate to each type.

2. For accounting purposes, the distinction between a *purchase* and a *pooling of interests* is to be found in the attendant circumstances rather than in the designation of the transaction according to its legal form (such as a merger, an exchange of shares, a consolidation, or an issuance of stock for assets and businesses), or in the number of corporations which survive or emerge, or in other legal or tax considerations (such as the availability of surplus for dividends).

3. For accounting purposes, a *purchase* may be described as a business combination of two or more corporations in which an important part of the ownership interests in the acquired corporation or corporations is eliminated or in which other factors requisite to a pooling of interests are not present.

4. In contrast, a *pooling of interests* may be described for accounting

purposes as a business combination of two or more corporations in which the holders of substantially all of the ownership interests[1] in the constituent corporations become the owners of a single corporation which owns the assets and businesses of the constituent corporations, either directly or through one or more subsidiaries, and in which certain other factors discussed below are present. Such corporation may be one of the constituent corporations or it may be a new corporation. After a pooling of interests, the net assets of all of the constituent corporations will in a large number of cases be held by a single corporation. However, the continuance in existence of one or more of the constituent corporations in a subsidiary relationship to another of the constituents or to a new corporation does not prevent the combination from being a pooling of interests if no significant minority interest remains outstanding, and if there are important tax, legal, or economic reasons for maintaining the subsidiary relationship, such as the preservation of tax advantages, the preservation of franchises or other rights, the preservation of the position of outstanding debt securities, or the difficulty or costliness of transferring contracts, leases, or licenses.

5. In determining the extent to which a new ownership or a continuity of old ownership exists in a particular business combination, consideration should be given to attendant circumstances. When the shares of stock that are received by the several owners of one of the predecessor corporations are not substantially in proportion to their respective interests in such predecessor, a new ownership or purchase of the predecessor is presumed to result. Similarly, if relative voting rights, as between the constituents, are materially altered through the issuance of senior equity or debt securities having limited or no voting rights, a purchase may be indicated. Likewise, a plan or firm intention and understanding to retire a substantial part of the capital stock issued to the owners of one or more of the constituent corporations, or substantial changes in ownership occurring shortly before or planned to occur shortly after the combination, tends to indicate that the combination is a purchase. However, where a constituent corporation has had two or more classes of stock outstanding prior to the origin of the

---

[1] As used in this bulletin, the term "ownership interests" refers basically to common stock, although in some cases the term may also include other classes of stock having senior or preferential rights as well as classes whose rights may be restricted in certain respects.

plan of combination, the redemption, retirement, or conversion of a class or classes of stock having senior or preferential rights as to assets and dividends need not prevent the combination from being considered to be a pooling of interests.

6. Other attendant circumstances should also be taken into consideration in determining whether a purchase or a pooling of interests is involved. Since the assumption underlying the pooling-of-interests concept is one of continuity of all of the constituents in one business enterprise, abandonment or sale of a large part of the business of one or more of the constituents militates against considering the combination as a pooling of interests. Similarly, the continuity of management or the power to control management is involved. Thus, if the management of one of the constituents is eliminated or its influence upon the over-all management of the enterprise is very small, a purchase may be indicated. Relative size of the constituents may not necessarily be determinative, especially where the smaller corporation contributes desired management personnel; however, where one of the constituent corporations is clearly dominant (for example, where the stockholders of one of the constituent corporations obtain 90% to 95% or more of the voting interest in the combined enterprise), there is a presumption that the transaction is a purchase rather than a pooling of interests.

7. No one of the factors discussed in paragraphs 5 and 6 would necessarily be determinative and any one factor might have varying degrees of significance in different cases. However, their presence or absence would be cumulative in effect. Since the conclusions to be drawn from consideration of these different relevant circumstances may be in conflict or partially so, determination as to whether a particular combination is a purchase or a pooling of interests should be made in the light of all such attendant circumstances.

8. When a combination is deemed to be a purchase, the assets acquired should be recorded on the books of the acquiring corporation at cost, measured in money, or, in the event other consideration is given, at the fair value of such other consideration, or at the fair value of the property acquired, whichever is more clearly evident. This is in accordance with the procedure applicable to accounting for purchases of assets.

9. When a combination is deemed to be a pooling of interests, a new basis of accountability does not arise. The carrying amounts of the assets of the constituent corporations, if stated in conformity with

generally accepted accounting principles and appropriately adjusted when deemed necessary to place them on a uniform accounting basis, should be carried forward; and the combined earned surpluses and deficits, if any, of the constituent corporations should be carried forward, except to the extent otherwise required by law or appropriate corporate action. Adjustments of assets or of surplus which would be in conformity with generally accepted accounting principles in the absence of a combination are ordinarily equally appropriate if effected in connection with a pooling of interests; however, the pooling-of-interests concept implies a combining of surpluses and deficits of the constituent corporations, and it would be inappropriate and misleading in connection with a pooling of interests to eliminate the deficit of one constituent against its capital surplus and to carry forward the earned surplus of another constituent.

10. Where one or more of the constituent corporations continues in existence in a subsidiary relationship, and the requirements of a pooling of interests have been met, the combination of earned surpluses in the consolidated balance sheet is proper since a pooling of interests is not an acquisition as that term is used in paragraph 3 of chapter 1(a) of *Accounting Research Bulletin No. 43* which states that earned surplus of a subsidiary corporation created prior to acquisition does not form a part of the consolidated earned surplus. Under the pooling-of-interests concept, the new enterprise is regarded as a continuation of all the constituent corporations and this holds true whether it is represented by a single corporation or by a parent corporation and one or more subsidiaries. If, however, prior to the origin of a plan of combination one party to the combination had been acquired by another such party as a subsidiary in circumstances which precluded the transactions from being considered a pooling of interests, the parent's share of the earned surplus of the subsidiary prior to such acquisition should not be included in the earned surplus of the pooled corporations.

11. Because of the variety of conditions under which a pooling of interests may be carried out, it is not practicable to deal with the accounting presentation except in general terms. A number of problems will arise. For example, if a single corporation survives in a pooling of interests, the stated capital of such corporation may be either more or less than the total of the stated capitals of the constituent corporations. In the former event, the excess may be deducted first from the total of any other contributed capital (capital surplus), and next from

the total of any earned surplus, of the constituent corporations. When the stated capital of the surviving corporation is less than the combined stated capital of the constituent corporations, the difference should appear in the balance sheet of the surviving corporation as other contributed capital (capital surplus), analogous to that created by a reduction in stated capital where no combination is involved.

12. When a combination is considered to be a pooling of interests, statements of operations issued by the continuing business for the period in which the combination occurs should ordinarily include the combined results of operations of the constituent interests for the part of the period preceding the date on which the combination was effected; if combined statements are not furnished, statements for the constituent corporations prior to the date of combination should be furnished separately or in appropriate groups. Results of operations of the several constituents during periods prior to that in which the combination was effected, when presented for comparative purposes, may be stated on a combined basis, or shown separately where, under the circumstances of the case, that presentation is more useful and informative. Disclosure that a business combination has been, or in the case of a proposed combination will be, treated as a pooling of interests should be made and any combined statements clearly described as such.

The statement entitled "Business Combinations" was unanimously adopted by the twenty-one members of the committee.

Notes

(See introduction to *Accounting Research Bulletin No. 43*.)

1. *Accounting Research Bulletins represent the considered opinion of at least two-thirds of the members of the committee on accounting procedure, reached on a formal vote after examination of the subject matter by the committee and the research department. Except in cases in which formal adoption by the Institute membership has been asked and secured, the authority of the bulletins rests upon the general acceptability of opinions so reached.*

2. *Opinions of the committee are not intended to be retroactive unless they contain a statement of such intention. They should not be*

considered applicable to the accounting for transactions arising prior to the publication of the opinions. However, the committee does not wish to discourage the revision of past accounts in an individual case if the accountant thinks it desirable in the circumstances. Opinions of the committee should be considered as applicable only to items which are material and significant in the relative circumstances.

3. It is recognized also that any general rules may be subject to exception; it is felt, however, that the burden of justifying departure from accepted procedures must be assumed by those who adopt other treatment. Except where there is a specific statement of a different intent by the committee, its opinions and recommendations are directed primarily to business enterprises organized for profit.

COMMITTEE ON ACCOUNTING PROCEDURE (1956-1957)

WILLIAM W. WERNTZ, *Chairman*	WILLARD J. GRAHAM	WILLIAM J. VON MINDEN
GORDON S. BATTELLE	NEWMAN T. HALVORSON	ROSS T. WARNER
GARRETT T. BURNS	DONALD R. JENNINGS	EDWARD B. WILCOX
DIXON FAGERBERG, JR.	HOMER L. LUTHER	JAMES B. WILLING
L. T. FLATLEY	JOHN K. MCCLARE	
THOMAS D. FLYNN	HERBERT E. MILLER	
CARL H. FORSBERG	JOHN PEOPLES	CARMAN G. BLOUGH
LEVERNE W. GARCIA	WELDON POWELL	*Director of Research*
	WALTER R. STAUB	

Selected Bibliography

The items listed below were selected primarily for their relevance to this research project. No attempt has been made to trace ideas to their sources or to compile a definitive bibliography on business combinations. With a few exceptions, general reference works, including textbooks and handbooks, have been omitted.

Accountants' Handbook, second edition, W. A. PATON, editor, section 17, pp. 949-50, "Effect of reorganizations on surplus." The Ronald Press Company. 1932.

Accountants' Handbook, third edition, W. A. PATON, editor, section 18, p. 1019, "Merger." The Ronald Press Company. 1943.

Accounting and Auditing Problems, CARMAN G. BLOUGH, editor, *The Journal of Accountancy.* "A practical merger problem," April 1949, pp. 343-45; "Summary of facts and comments concerning a recent merger," July 1949, pp. 82-84; "Treatment of surplus upon parent's liquidation of subsidiary," April 1950, pp. 352-53; "Treatment of excess of consideration paid over net assets acquired," April 1952, pp. 472-73; "Carrying earned surplus forward in a pooling of interests," June 1954, pp. 708-9; "Business combination: 'pooling' or purchase?" July 1957, pp. 55-56. Portions of several of Mr. Blough's regular columns on accounting and auditing problems dealt with practical issues in the combination area, generally in reply to questions submitted by readers.

Accounting at the SEC, LOUIS RAPPAPORT, editor, *New York Certified Public Accountant.* "Business combinations," June 1959, pp. 449-50; "Combination of purchase and pooling," July 1959, pp. 528-29.

AMERICAN INSTITUTE OF CERTIFIED PUBLIC ACCOUNTANTS, *Accounting Research Bulletin No. 43,* "Restatement and Revision of Accounting Research Bulletins," chapter 1a, "Rules adopted by membership." 1953.

BARR, ANDREW, "Accounting aspects of business combinations," *Accounting Review,* April 1959, pp. 175-81. A good historical treatment of the accounting problems in the business combination area, with an indication of the thinking of the Securities and Exchange Commission in its determination of the appropriateness of the accounting for combinations. Herein lie some clues as to how the present status of accounting for combinations came to be.

BLACK, WILLIAM M., "Certain phases of merger accounting," *The Journal of Accountancy*, March 1947, pp. 214-20. An early discussion in which a clear distinction is drawn between an acquisition (purchase) and a merger (pooling).

BUTTERS, J. KEITH, LINTNER, JOHN, and CARY, WILLIAM L., *Effects of Taxation; Corporate Mergers*. Division of Research, Graduate School of Business Administration, Harvard University. 1951. A thorough treatment of the various factors motivating both the buying and selling interests in a business combination, with emphasis placed upon the effects of various tax-law provisions. The general conclusion is that tax pressures are likely quite influential but are rarely the prime motivation.

FULD, JAMES J., "Some practical aspects of a merger," *Harvard Law Review*, Sept. 1947, pp. 1092-1118. A concise discussion of the accounting for mergers appearing at an early date. Critical attention is directed to the possible future effect upon dividends as a result of the accounting action taken for a business combination.

GRAICHEN, RAYMOND E., "Buying and selling a corporate business," *The Journal of Accountancy*, April 1959, pp. 45-53. A discussion of why stockholders sell their business and why purchasers buy, including a discussion of three nontaxable routes by which a corporation may sell or transfer the ownership of assets and business to another corporation.

HARRIS, WILLIAM B., "The urge to merge," *Fortune*, Nov. 1954, pp. 102-106, 236, 238, 240, and 242. An historical development of the merger movements in this country with emphasis placed upon the various motivations which stimulated these movements.

In the matter of The Montana Power Company, United States Federal Power Commission. *Opinions and Decisions of the Federal Power Commission*, vol. 4, Oct. 1, 1943-Dec. 31, 1945. United States Government Printing Office. 1946.

KAPLAN, A. D. H., "The current merger movement analyzed," *Harvard Business Review*, May-June 1955, pp. 91-100. A historical development of the merger movements in this country with emphasis upon the social and economic considerations within which the movements developed. Emphasis is placed upon the effect which mergers have upon lessening of competition.

KRIPKE, HOMER, "A good look at goodwill in corporate acquisitions," *Banking Law Journal*, Dec. 1961, pp. 1028-40.

Legal, Financial, and Tax Aspects of Mergers and Acquisitions, ELIZABETH MARTING, editor. Financial Management Series 114. American Management Association, Inc. 1957. A monograph containing articles by several writers on the legal, financial, and tax aspects of combinations. Of particular interest are the articles by James B. Walker, Jr., Hugh M. McNeill, John M. Gwynne, and M. A. Adelman.

LENT, GEORGE E., "Net operating loss carryovers and corporate mergers," *Tax Executive*, April 1959, pp. 241-69. A discussion of how the provisions of the Internal Revenue Code of 1954 have contributed to the widespread growth in the corporate merger movement, with particular emphasis on the impact of the net operating loss carryover provision.

MAY, GEORGE O., "Business combinations: an alternate view," *The Journal of Accountancy*, April 1957, pp. 33-36. A historical review of the development of the concept of "pooling of interests" and a suggestion that in a pooling the current values inherent in *all* the assets in the combination are of prime significance. Mr. May feels the more closely the monetary ascriptions of the assets reflect the effective cost to present-day stockholders of their interest in the surviving company the more significant and useful these amounts will be.

Mergers and Acquisitions. Published for distribution at AMA Special Finance Conference, Oct. 16-18, 1957. American Management Association, Inc. 1957. A monograph containing several interesting articles concerning various aspects of mergers, including their propriety, the tax considerations, alternative diversification approaches. Articles by Edgar T. Mead, Jr., Charles H. Welling, and John C. J. Wirth, and Matthew F. Blake are particularly good.

MOONITZ, MAURICE, "*The Basic Postulates of Accounting.*" Accounting Research Study No. 1, American Institute of Certified Public Accountants. 1961.

MOONITZ, MAURICE, and STAEHLING, CHARLES C., *Accounting: An Analysis of Its Problems*, vol. 2, Chapter 31. Foundation Press. 1952. A discussion of accounting for business combinations and an introduction to the concept of an "organic merger." The Celanese-Tubize merger forms the basis for the discussion, which is the most thorough of that appearing in any of the standard accounting textbooks.

Niagara Falls Power Co. v. Federal Power Commission, July 29, 1943. *137 Federal Reporter, 2d Series.* West Publishing Co. 1943.

SCHRADER, WILLIAM J., "Business combinations," *Accounting Review*, Jan. 1958, pp. 72-75. An article which emphasizes the extreme importance of a proper determination of the appropriate accounting entity in determination of the appropriate accounting for business combinations.

UNITED STATES FEDERAL TRADE COMMISSION. *Report on Corporate Mergers, 1951-54.* 1955. The results of a study by the Federal Trade Commission of the motivations behind corporate mergers and the impact of such mergers on the economy. The report is presented within the framework of the various regulations regarding restraint of trade and with consideration of the effects of combinations upon third parties and competition generally.

WERNTZ, WILLIAM W., "Corporate consolidations, reorganizations and mergers," *New York Certified Public Accountant*, July 1945, pp. 379-87, One of the earliest detailed discussions of the concepts of purchase and pooling in which emphasis is placed on the end results of the combination transaction rather than upon the legal form in which the transaction may be consummated. Many of the issues discussed in some depth remain unsettled at the present time.

WERNTZ, WILLIAM W., "Intangibles in business combinations," *The Journal of Accountancy*, May 1957, pp. 46-50. An excellent article relating the various issues of accounting for intangibles to the business combinations problem. Many important questions pertinent to the combination area are discussed and suggestions for resolving these questions are presented.

WESTON, FRANK T., "Recent developments in accounting practice," *Arthur Young Journal*, Oct. 1960, pp. 1-6.

WILCOX, EDWARD B., "Business combinations: an analysis of mergers, purchases, and related accounting procedure," *The Journal of Accountancy*, Feb. 1950, pp. 102-7. An article setting forth the most complete discussion of the various criteria of significance in determining the nature of a business combination which had appeared up to that time. Several of the practical problems to be faced in accounting for business combinations are also set forth along with several deviations in existing practice.

WILDMAN, JOHN R., and POWELL, WELDON, *Capital Stock Without Par Value.* A. W. Shaw Company. 1928.

Index

Accounting entity, 71, 72, 78, 80
Accounting Research Bulletin No. 24, 38
Accounting Research Bulletin No. 40, 12, 24, 25, 27, 32, 35, 37
Accounting Research Bulletin No. 43, Chapter 5, 31, 32, 38, 39, 59, 64, 88, 105
Accounting Research Bulletin No. 43, Chapter 7c, 12, 28, 30, 32, 35, 50
Accounting Research Bulletin No. 48, 13, 28, 33, 34, 35, 37, 38, 41, 42, 50, 51, 53, 54, 61, 73, 79, 94, 102, 104, 110, 111, 113
Aluminum Company of America, 51, 52
American Machine & Foundry Co., 49, 50, 51
American Smelting and Refining Company, 2
Antitrust legislation, 8, 9
Arm's-length bargaining, 20, 21, 22, 72, 73, 99, 101
Asset book values, carry forward of, 19, 20, 21
Asset values, changing nature of, 81, 82, 92
Assets, accounting for, 17, 18, 30, 31, 74, 105
Attendant circumstances, 25, 35, 83

Bargain purchases, 97
Bargaining position, 95, 96
Bell & Howell Company, 47, 48
Business combination
    Defined, 12, 69, 104
    Nature of, 69, 70, 109
    Types of, 9, 10, 11

Caterpillar Tractor Co., 24, 29
Celanese Corporation of America, 24
Clayton Act, 1, 9
Committee on public utility accounting, 23
Consideration given, accounting for, 77, 78, 79, 80
Continuity of equity interests criterion, 35, 36

Disclosure
    Nature of the transaction, 45, 46, 53, 54
    "Pooled" combinations, 43, 44
    "Purchased" combinations, 44, 45
Diversification, 6, 8

Earned surplus
    See Retained earnings
Earnings per share, 88, 89, 90, 94, 95, 96, 105
    Dilution of, 88, 89, 90
Estate tax, 6
Exchange transaction, 68, 69, 70, 71, 72, 73, 75, 80, 93

Fair value pooling concept, 15, 74, 81, 82, 83, 84, 107
Federal Power Commission, 22
Fifty per cent-owned company, 100
Food Machinery and Chemical Corporation, 53
"Fresh start," 77, 85, 107, 108

General Telephone & Electronics Corporation, 44
Glen Alden Corporation, 47
Goodwill
  Accounting for, 16, 58, 59, 60, 62, 87, 106, 113
  Allocation of excess to, 31, 62, 63, 106
  Amortization of, 32, 59, 60, 62, 64, 88, 89, 98, 105, 106, 114
  Growth, 7, 60

The Hecht Co., 48

Income tax, influence of, 4, 6, 7, 16, 39, 41, 57
Intangibles, the problem of, 16, 38
Investment bankers, 2, 3, 4

Legal entity, 79
Lenkurt Electric Co., Inc., 44

The May Department Stores, 48
Merger period
  First, 2
  Recent, 4
  Second, 3
Minority interest, 102, 113
Morris 5 & 10 Cent to $1 Stores, Inc., 32
Multi-step combinations, 100
G. C. Murphy, 32

National City Lines Inc., 45

The Ohio Oil Company, 45
Operating-loss carryover, 6, 7

Pooling, fair value
  See Fair value pooling
Pooling of interests, 5, 15, 19, 22, 23, 24, 25, 36, 45, 46, 56, 57, 60, 62, 84, 109, 110
Pooling-of-interests accounting, 14, 15, 23, 24, 55, 56, 71, 76, 99, 105
  Consequences of, 92-96
  Problems arising from adoption of, 98-102

Pooling of interests, AICPA criteria for, 25, 26, 35, 36, 73, 104, 110
Poolings
  See Pooling of interests
Preferred stock in combinations, use of, 36, 52, 101, 111, 112
Pro forma statements, 47
Pullman Incorporated, 46
Purchase accounting, 14, 25, 71, 74, 77, 78
  Consequences of, 87-92
  Problems arising from adoption of, 96-98
Purchases, 5, 15, 54, 60, 109, 110

Quasi-reorganization, 84, 85

Raytheon Company, 52, 53
Recasting of prior year data, 46, 48, 107
Relative size criterion, 28, 35, 50, 51, 73, 110
Retained earnings
  Accounting for, 32, 64, 78, 92, 105
  Carry forward of, 19, 20, 21
  Direct write-off to, 30, 38, 59, 92, 93, 114
Retroactive change of accounting treatment, 49, 50, 51, 55, 66, 67
Rexall Drug and Chemical Company, 47

Secret reserves, 5
Sherman Act, 1, 8, 9
Sorensen & Company, 52, 53
Standard Oil Company, 2
Statutory mergers, 10, 39
Subsidiary, continuance of acquired company as a, 37
Sunray Mid-Continent Oil Company, 46
Surplus available for dividends, 33, 65, 66, 80, 85
Sylvania Electric Products Inc., 44

"Tax-free" exchanges, 5, 16, 39, **40**, 41, 58, 60, 105

145

Trackson Co., 24, 29
Treasury stock, 111, 112, 113
Tubize Rayon Corporation, 24

Union Carbide and Carbon Corporation, 29, 30

Union Tank Car Company, 47
United States Steel Corporation, 2

Visking Corporation, 29

Watered stock, 2, 4, 5